AGES 6-8

SUPER SIMPLE BIBLE LESSONS

60 Ready-to-Use Bible Activities

Abingdon Press

Nashville

Abingdon's
SUPER SIMPLE BIBLE LESSONS
60 Ready–to–Use Bible Activities
Ages 6–8

Copyright ©2005 Abingdon Press
All rights reserved

No part of this work, EXCEPT patterns and pages covered by the notice below, may be repro-
duced or transmitted in any form or by any means, electronic or mechanical, including photo-
copying and recording, or by any information storage or retrieval system, except as may be
expressly permitted by the 1976 Copyright Act or by permission in writing from the publisher.
Requests for permission should be submitted in writing to:
Abingdon Press, 201 Eighth Avenue South, Nashville, TN 37203,
faxed to (615) 749-6128, or submitted via email to *permissions@abingdonpress.com*.

Notice
ONLY patterns and activity pages that contain the copyright notice may be duplicated
for use in the local church or church school.
The following copyright notice is included on these pages and must appear on the reproduction:

**Permission to photocopy for local church use.
©2005 Abingdon Press.**

Unless otherwise noted, Scripture quotations in this publication are from the New Revised
Standard Version of the Bible, copyrighted ©1989 by the Division of Christian Education of the
National Council of the Churches of Christ in the United States of America, and are used by per-
mission. All rights reserved.

Scripture quotations that are labeled CEV are from the Contemporary English Version, ©1991,
1992, 1995 by the American Bible Society. Used by permission.

ISBN 9780687497805

Art by Megan Jeffery, with the exception of p. 71 by Susan Harrison © 2005 Abingdon Press.

09 10 11 12 13 14—10 9 8 7 6 5 4 3

MANUFACTURED IN THE UNITED STATES OF AMERICA

TABLE OF CONTENTS

How to use this resource

Sometimes all you need is a Bible story that is ready to tell and a simple craft or game that requires almost nothing at all to do it. If you've ever heard yourself say this, then this resource is for you!

Super Simple Bible Lessons is a quick trip through the Bible, from Genesis to the letters of Paul. Each lesson contains these elements:

1. A Bible story
2. A Bible verse to memorize
3. A Bible story-related activity (craft or game)

At the back of the book is a scripture index if you would like to coordinate the stories here with other stories you may be using with the children. Also available from Abingdon Press is a corresponding resource for preschoolers.

The activities included in this resource require minimal supplies, most of which are available to you in the typical church school classroom, or they may be easily obtained from the church office.

Basic Supplies

printer paper	white glue	crayons or markers
construction paper	masking tape	paper fasteners
string or yarn	paper punch	stapler, staples
scissors	pencils	wooden craft sticks
cardboard	posterboard	paper plates
baby oil	cotton swabs	sandpaper
cardboard tubes	art tissue	small containers
recycled newspaper	envelopes	rubber bands
aluminum foil	fabric scraps	ribbon
shoeboxes	coins	plastic drinking straws

THE BEGINNING

The Bible
Genesis 1:1-19

The heavens are telling
the glory of God.
(Psalm 19:1)

Supplies
glue
paper
stapler
staples
string or yarn
scissors
paper punch
construction
   paper
white crayon,
   white chalk, or
   glitter glue

Bible Story
It was dark, so very dark,
As dark as the darkest night.
Then a wind from God passed over,
And God said, "Let there be light."
The light began to glimmer;
The light began to shine.
Once there was only darkest dark,
Now light and dark aligned.

God put the light on one side,
And the dark was on the other.
"Day and night, now that's a start
To clean up all this clutter."
Then God looked 'round the empty sky
And said, "Let there be different lights.
A brighter one for daytime,
and a lesser one for nights.

"Let lights shine down upon the earth
Down through the stratosphere.
These lights will mark the day and night,
The seasons and the years.
Then fill up all that empty space
With balls of fire called stars.
Let planets travel 'round the sun—
Saturn, Jupiter, and Mars."

Then God looked down on all that was
And saw that it was good.
The lights that God created,
Were doing what they should.
The dark that once was darkest dark
Now glowed with awesome light.
There was sunlight in the daytime,
And a moon and stars at night.

creative FUN

1. Make a copy of these figures and directions.
2. Cut black construction paper into 1-inch by 11-inch strips. For each mobile, you will need four strips.
3. Lay two of the strips across each other forming a "+". Staple in the center where the two pieces cross.
4. Place the other two strips end to end and staple, forming one long strip.
5. Write the Bible verse along the end-to-end strip. Use white crayon, white chalk, or glitter glue.
6. Join the ends of the long strip to form a circle.
7. Glue or staple the ends of the "+" onto the circle.
8. Punch holes along the bottom edge of the circle.
9. Tape yarn or string to each of the "heavenly bodies" above.
10. Tie the figures to the circle.

Permission to photocopy for local church use. ©2004 Abingdon Press.

FILLING THE EARTH

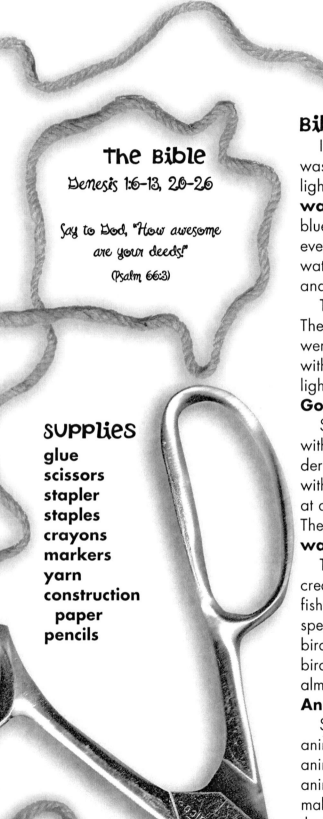

the Bible
Genesis 1:6–13, 20–26

Say to God, "How awesome are your deeds!"

(Psalm 66:3)

supplies
**glue
scissors
stapler
staples
crayons
markers
yarn
construction
 paper
pencils**

Bible story

In the beginning, before there was anything else, there was darkness. **And there was God.** Then God created light. There was darkness and there was light. **And there was God.** God divided the sky from the sea. There was blue sky and orange sky and purple sky and sky that was every color you could imagine. There was rolling water, deep water, cold water, dark water. There was light and darkness and water and sky. **And there was God.**

Then from the water God caused dry land to appear. There were great high mountains and hot, dry deserts. There were rolling hills and wide prairies. There were seashores with sandy beaches. There was darkness, and there was light. There was sky and sea and earth. **And there was God.**

Still God was not finished. God created plants—plants with thick green leaves, plants with wooden trunks and tender stems, plants with prickly thorns and tasty fruits, plants with big flowers and plants with flowers you can hardly see at all. There was darkness and light. There was sky and sea. There was earth filled with growing things. **And there was God.**

The world was such an empty place. There were no living creatures to enjoy it. So God created fish—big fish, little fish, short and fat fish, long and skinny fish, striped fish, speckled fish, prickly fish, and slimy fish. Then God created birds—big birds, little birds, short and fat birds, tall and thin birds, birds with short legs, birds with long legs, birds with almost no legs at all. There were fish, and there were birds. **And there was God.**

Still something was missing. God created animals—big animals, little animals, short and fat animals, tall and thin animals. There were animals that walked, animals that ran, animals that flew, and animals that crawled. There were animals that hopped and swam and slithered. There were animals that hardly moved at all. There were animals all over the place. **And there was God.**

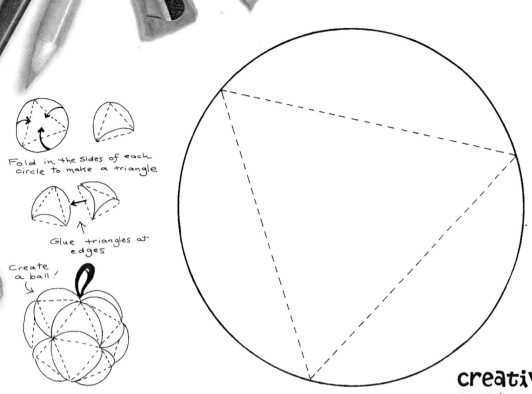

Fold in the sides of each circle to make a triangle

Glue triangles at edges

Create a ball!

creative fun

1. Make copies of the circle with the triangle, the diagram on how to assemble the figure, and the animals.
2. Using the circle as a pattern, cut ten circles from construction paper.
3. Using the triangle as a pattern, trace the triangle in the center of each circle.
4. Let the children color the animals.
5. Cut apart the various animals. Glue one animal in the center of each triangle. (Children may draw their own animal if they prefer.)
6. Crease the three traced lines on each circle and fold the three flaps upward.
7. Staple or glue the flaps on five circles together as shown to form the top of the ball. Repeat with five circles for the bottom of the ball.
8. Add yarn for a hanger.

Permission to photocopy for local church use. © 1997, 2000 Abingdon Press.

IN GOD'S IMAGE

The Bible

Genesis 1:26–27, 31

So God created humankind in his image.

(Genesis 1:27)

Supplies

paper
pencils
markers
scissors
white glue
construction
   paper

Bible Story

Even though there was now night and day, land and sea, plants and all varieties of living creatures, God knew that the world was not finished yet.

God said, "There are all kinds of living things doing what living things are supposed to do. But there are no living things who can enjoy all that I have put on the earth. There are no living things who can think or plan for the future. There are no living things who can imagine or create. There are no living things who know the difference between right and wrong."

So God created human beings—male and female. God made them in God's own image and blessed them.

God made people in different sizes and shapes. God made people in different colors. God made people with different likes and dislikes. God made people who could do different things. God made women and men, boys and girls.

God made artists and musicians. God made planners and builders. God made writers and readers. God made preachers and teachers. God made runners and swimmers. God made baseball players and computer operators. And God made YOU!

God made a world full of people—all in the image of God and yet different from one another. And God looked down on all that had been created and said, "This is very good."

Creative Fun

1. Make a copy of the mirror on the following page, one for each child.
2. Cut out the mirror and glue it onto construction paper.
3. Write things on the mirror that show how you reflect the image of God. For example, "When I help others."
4. Share your mirrors with one another.

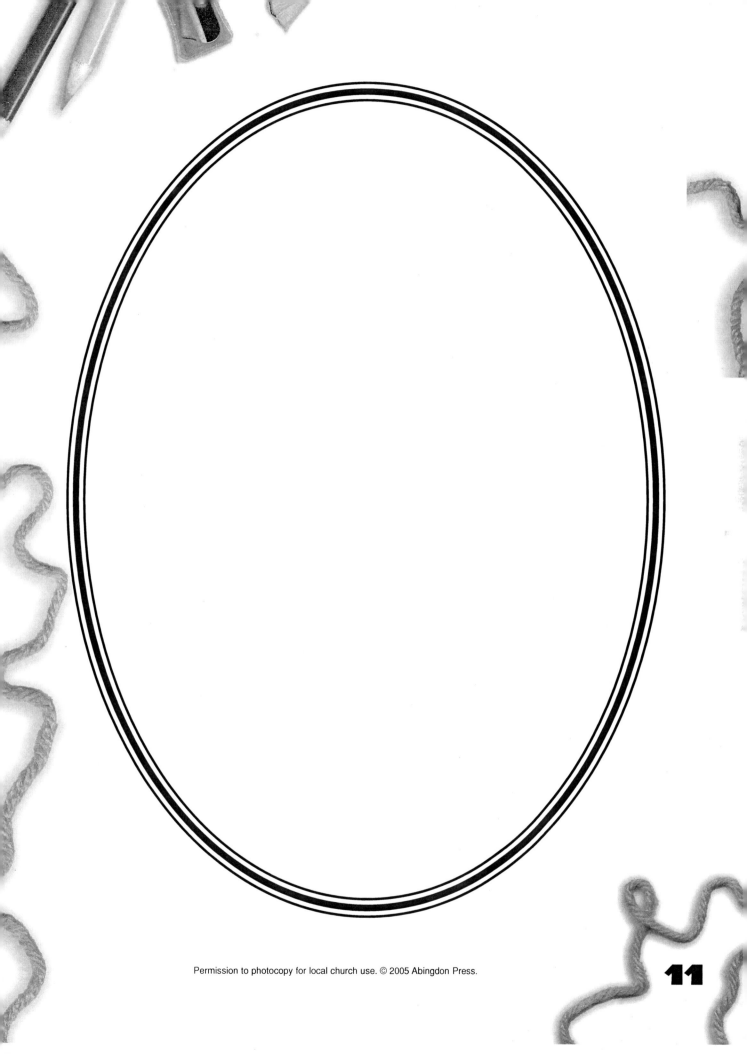

Permission to photocopy for local church use. © 2005 Abingdon Press.

NOAH

The Bible

Genesis 6:5—9:17

Our Lord, you bless everyone who lives right and obeys your law.

(Psalm 119:1, CEV)

Supplies

glue
paper
scissors
crayons
markers
wooden craft
   sticks
construction
   paper
masking tape

Bible Story

In the beginning, God created a world. God filled this world with plants, birds, fish, and animals of every sort. God filled the world with people. And everything was good.

The people remembered God. They talked with God. They thanked God for all the wonderful things God had given them. But after a while, the people forgot. They forgot who had created them and all the world around them. All the people forgot about God—all except Noah and his family.

One day God spoke to Noah, "Noah!"

Noah looked around. He did not see anyone standing near him. Then he heard the voice again.

"Noah, this is God." Now Noah was frightened. "I'm not happy with the way things are on the earth. The people mistreat one another. They are unkind. They are disrespectful—except for you and your family. I want to start all over again."

Noah waited for God to say something else.

"Noah, I am going to send a great flood. I want you to build a boat—a very big boat."

So, in a land far away from the sea, Noah and his family set about building a very big boat. When his neighbors saw what he was doing, they made fun of him, but Noah did not listen to them. He just kept building. Noah was faithful to God.

When the boat was finally finished, God said, "Noah, I want you to fill the boat with animals, two of every kind on earth." So Noah gathered animals to go into the boat. There were elephants and kangaroos, tigers and chimpanzees, rhinoceros and giraffes, parakeets and camels, fleas and butterflies, snails and rabbits, turtles and alligators. There were so many animals that Noah lost count.

When everyone and everything was safe inside the boat, the rain began to fall. It rained for forty days and forty nights, but Noah and his family and all the animals were safe inside.

When the rain stopped and the waters went down, God told Noah it was time to leave the ark. Up in the sky was a rainbow, a sign of God's promise never to destroy the earth again, and we can depend on God's promises.

Tape craft stick to the back of the ark!

Let ark "sail" under the wave strip!

creative Fun
1. Make a copy of the ark for each child
2. Cut out the boat and the waves.
3. Color with crayons or markers.
4. Tape a craft stick to the back of the boat.
5. Staple or glue the waves onto a piece of construction paper, leaving the center area free.
6. Slip the boat between the waves and the construction paper.
7. Move the craft stick and Noah's ark will ride the waves.

Permission to photocopy for local church use. © 2003 Abingdon Press.

A BLESSING TO ALL

The Bible

Genesis 12:1-3; 13:14-16; 15:1-6

How precious is your steadfast love, O God!

(Psalm 36:7)

Supplies

glue
paper
cardboard
tubes
black
construction
paper
tape
shapened pencil,
push pin, or
toothpick
scissors
pencils

Bible Story

Abraham and Sarah lived in a country far away. They had many sheep and goats, but they did not have any children.

One day God spoke to Abraham, "I want you to leave your home and go to a land that I will show you. If you do this, I will give you many children and grandchildren. I will make your name a blessing to all people."

Sarah and Abraham were very old. They didn't want to leave their home and their friends. **But Abraham and Sarah trusted God**. So they packed up all their belongings. Then they set off to the new land that God would show them.

All along the way they would stop to let their animals eat. Sometimes Abraham and Sarah missed their home. They did not know where God was leading them. **But Abraham and Sarah trusted God.**

One day they came to a beautiful land. God said, "Some day all this land will belong to your children and to their children." Abraham and Sarah knew they they didn't have any children yet. **But Abraham and Sarah trusted God.**

Later God said to Abraham. "Don't be afraid. I will protect you and reward you greatly." But Abraham was beginning to doubt.

"Lord, you have given Sarah and I everything we could ask for, except children. We still have no children to inherit this land that you have promised."

And God said, "Look at the sky and see if you can count the stars. That's how many descendants you will have." **But Abraham and Sarah trusted God.**

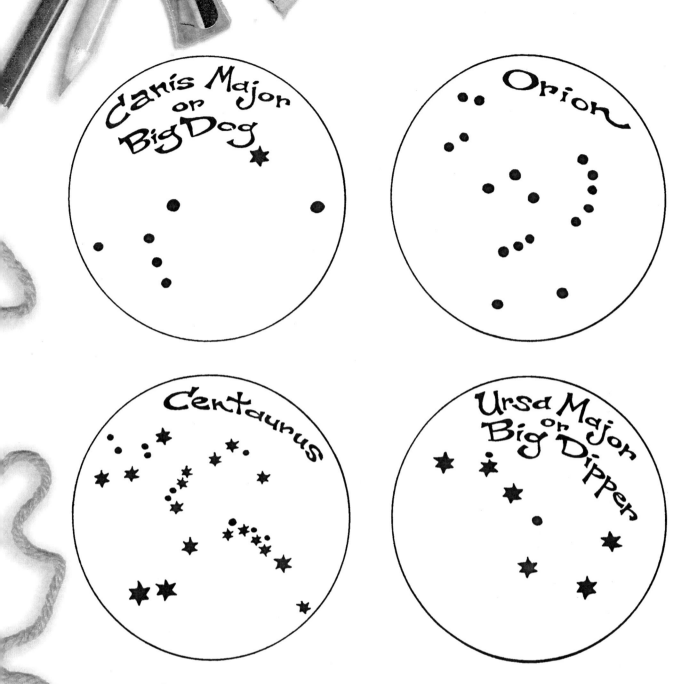

CREATIVE FUN

1. Make a copy of the constellations for each child.
2. Cover a cardboard tube with black construction paper.
3. Cut out the four constellation circles.
4. Place the constellation circles onto a piece of black construction paper. Trace around them. Cut out the circles from the construction paper.
5. Place each constellation over a black circle. Use tape to hold it in place.
6. Use a sharpened pencil, a toothpick, or a push pin to poke a hole at each place where a star is drawn.
7. Hold the cardboard tube up to your eye. Place the constellation circle in front of the other end.
8. Think about how God promised Abraham and Sarah that their children would outnumber the stars.

Permission to photocopy for local church use. © 1999 Abingdon Press.

SARAH LAUGHS

The Bible
Genesis 18:1-15; 21:1-3

Is anything too wonderful for the Lord?

(Genesis 18:14)

Supplies
glue
paper
cardboard
scissors
crayons
markers
sandpaper

Bible Story
Ha, ha, ha. Ho, ho, ho. He, he, he.
You'll never believe what's happened to me.

Abraham and Sarah settled in the land of Canaan. One day three strangers appeared at the tents. It was unusual for persons to travel about on foot this far from cities. There were deserts and rough roads and very little water. So Abraham and Sarah welcomed them warmly.

Ha, ha, ha. Ho, ho, ho. He, he, he.
You'll never believe what's happened to me.

Abraham rushed to greet the strangers. He invited them to sit beneath a tree and rest. He ran into the tent and asked Sarah to prepare a fine meal for them. Sarah prepared bread and meat and milk for them.

Ha, ha, ha. Ho, ho, ho. He, he, he.
You'll never believe what's happened to me.

When it came time for the three strangers to leave, one of them said to Abraham, "By this time next year, Sarah will have a son." Sarah heard what the man said. She laughed and laughed and laughed. She laughed because she was very old—too old to have a baby.

Ha, ha, ha. Ho, ho, ho. He, he, he.
You'll never believe what's happened to me.

The visitor heard Sarah laughing. "Sarah should know that nothing is too hard for God." And sure enough, just as the stranger had said, one year passed and Sarah and Abraham had a son. They named him Isaac, which means *he laughs.*

Creative Fun
1. Make a copy of the diorama figures for each child.
2. Cut cardboard into 12-inch squares. Paint with white glue and cover with sandpaper.
3. Color the figures. Cut them out. Fold on the dotted lines so that they will stand up.

4. Stand the figures on the sandpaper, arranging them to show the scene where the three strangers visited Abraham and Sarah.

Permission to photocopy for local church use. © 2000 Abingdon Press.

A WIFE FOR ISAAC

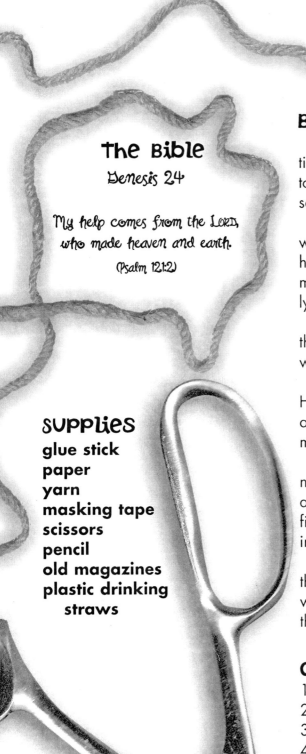

The Bible

Genesis 24

My help comes from the Lord, who made heaven and earth.

(Psalm 121:2)

Supplies

glue stick
paper
yarn
masking tape
scissors
pencil
old magazines
**plastic drinking
    straws**

Bible Story

When Isaac grew to be a man, his father decided it was time for him to be married, but Abraham didn't want Isaac to marry any of the girls in Canaan. So Abraham sent his servant back to their home town to find a wife for his son.

The servant was worried that he would not find the right wife for Isaac, so he asked God to help him be successful in his search. Across the wilderness the servant rode, with his many camels and gifts of gold. The servant wanted the family of the girl he chose to know that Abraham was very rich.

When the servant came to the town, he stopped to rest in the shade beside the village well. Women from the city would come to the well for water.

The servant asked one of the girls for a drink of water. Her name was Rebekah. She gave him water to drink. She also got water for his camels. The servant knew that she must be the one that God had chosen.

Rebekah invited the servant to stay with her family that night. The servant told Rebekah's family all about Abraham and his son Isaac. He told them how God had helped him find Rebekah. The servant asked if Rebekah would be willing to go back with him and marry Abraham's son Isaac.

Rebekah agreed to the marriage. Her family agreed to the marriage. The servant gave Rebekah and her family the wonderful gifts. Then Rebekah went back with the servant to the land of Canaan where she married Isaac.

Creative Fun

1. Make a copy of the triangle patterns for each child.
2. Tear out colorful pages from old magazines.
3. Trace triangles onto the magazine pages and cut out.
4. Turn the triangle face down and cover the back side with glue, using a glue stick.
5. Lay a plastic straw along the base of the triangle and roll, wrapping the paper around the straw. You can place several beads on one straw.

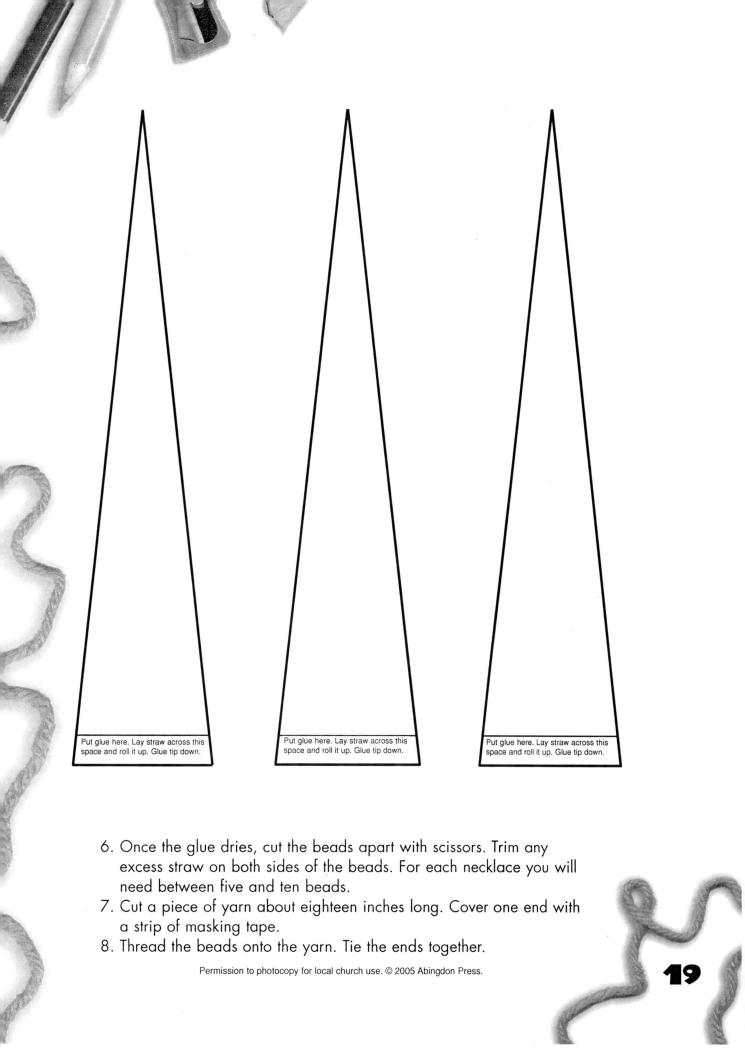

Put glue here. Lay straw across this space and roll it up. Glue tip down.

Put glue here. Lay straw across this space and roll it up. Glue tip down.

Put glue here. Lay straw across this space and roll it up. Glue tip down.

6. Once the glue dries, cut the beads apart with scissors. Trim any excess straw on both sides of the beads. For each necklace you will need between five and ten beads.

7. Cut a piece of yarn about eighteen inches long. Cover one end with a strip of masking tape.

8. Thread the beads onto the yarn. Tie the ends together.

Permission to photocopy for local church use. © 2005 Abingdon Press.

JACOB AND ESAU

The Bible

Genesis 25:27-34

For I have learned to be content with whatever I have.
(Philippians 4:11)

Supplies
glue
paper
posterboard
rubber bands
paper punch
scissors

Bible Story

Isaac and Rebekah beamed at the two babies with great pride. Just yesterday they had no children and were very lonely. Today they had two new sons.

Isaac smiled at one of the babies. The baby's skin was reddish, and he was covered with a fine silky hair. "I think we will call him Esau," said Isaac. (*Esau* sounded like the word for hairy.)

Rebekah stroked the other baby. His skin was fair and smooth. His hair was black as night and lay in soft little curls about his face. "We will call you Jacob," said Rebekah.

The two boys were twins, but no twins could have been as different as Esau and Jacob. Esau loved to play with swords and fought pretend soldiers. He had a small bow and arrow and often went hunting with his father.

Jacob liked music and quieter games. Rather than go into the hills with his brother, he stayed around the tents and cared for the sheep. He learned to cook and helped his mother.

As the boys grew older, their differences grew even more. One day Esau returned from a very long hunting trip. As he drew near the tents, he smelled something delicious. Esau rubbed his stomach and looked forward to a great bowl of stew that he was sure Jacob was cooking.

Now Jacob was a tricky boy. Because his brother had been born first, Esau would inherit almost all the family wealth. Jacob would get only a small amount. Jacob wondered if there wasn't something he could do about it.

When Esau rushed into the camp and demanded food, Jacob said, "I'll give you this bowl of stew, but you must give me your birthright as firstborn son."

"What good is a birthright if I starve to death this very day. It is done!" Esau snatched the bowl from his brother's hands. He began to gobble it up.

Jacob smiled to himself. "Esau may be older than I am, but he is not smarter." Jacob wondered what Esau would say when he realized what he had done.

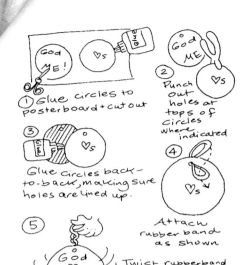

① Glue circles to posterboard + cut out

② Punch out holes at tops of circles where indicated

③ Glue circles back-to-back, making sure holes are lined up.

④ Attach rubber band as shown

⑤ Twist rubberband + watch the secret message appear!

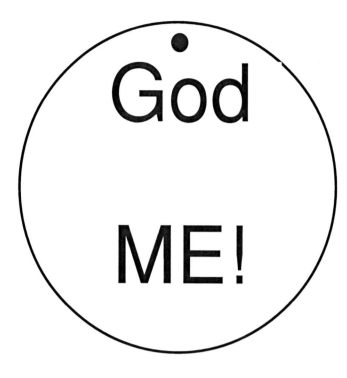

God
ME!

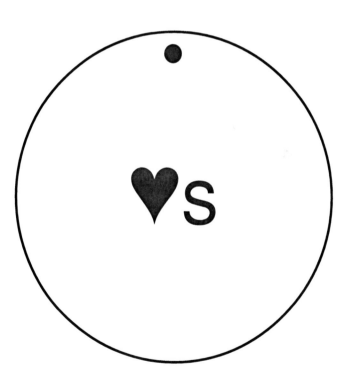

♥s

Permission to photocopy for local church use. © 2005 Abingdon Press.

JOSEPH'S COAT

The Bible

Genesis 37:1-28

But the LORD was with Joseph and showed him steadfast love. (Genesis 39:21)

Supplies

paper
crayons
scissors
markers
option: fabric
scraps

Bible Story

"Did you see what Father gave him this time?" asked Reuben, shaking his head.

"Yes, I did. Father doesn't give us impractical gifts like that. What is so special about Joseph anyway?" asked Gad.

The brothers knew that Joseph was their father's favorite son. Jacob was always doing special things for Joseph. This new gift made them very angry with their brother.

"A coat like that is bad for a boy who watches the sheep. Better to give him a new leather carry sack or a warm woolen mantle. Can you see Joseph chasing after sheep and goats in that long robe? Those long sleeves will catch on every thorn bush in the pasture," Simeon complained.

"As if father will send him into the fields at all," Dan mumbled under his breath.

This didn't bother Joseph one bit. He loved his new coat. It made him feel special just to put it on. He liked the soft wool. He liked the long, flowing sleeves. But Joseph could not understand why every time he put it on, his brothers grumbled and said unkind things to him.

One day Jacob sent Joseph out into the fields to find his brothers. They had been gone for a very long time. He wore his new coat. When the brothers saw him coming, they began to plan how to get rid of him.

When Joseph came into the camp, the brothers took his coat and threw Joseph into a deep pit. They planned to leave him there and tell Jacob that a wild animal had attacked and killed him.

But just then they had a better idea. They saw a caravan of Ishmaelites on their way to Egypt. "Let's get rid of Joseph and make some money at the same time." So they dragged Joseph from the pit and sold him as a slave to the Ishmaelites.

Little did the brothers know that God had a plan for Joseph. The spoiled brat who had made their lives miserable would one day save their family from starvation.

creative Fun

1. Make a copy of this page for each child.
2. Cut out the robe pattern and decorate it.
3. Create a special robe for Joseph.

Permission to photocopy for local church use. © 1998 Abingdon Press.

BABY IN A BASKET

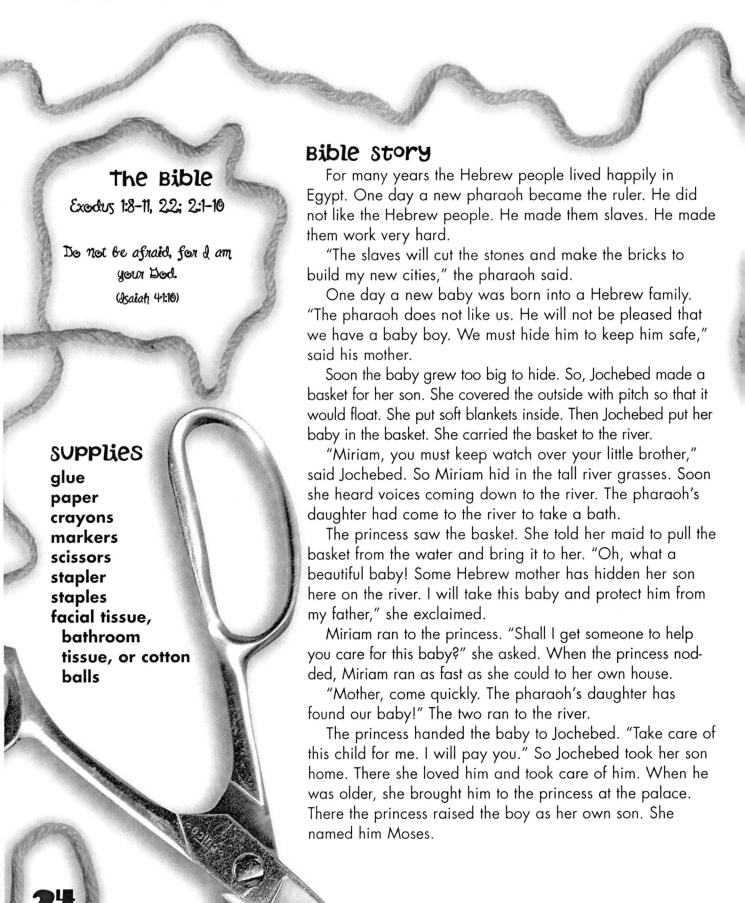

the Bible

Exodus 1:8-11, 22; 2:1-10

Do not be afraid, for I am your God.

(Isaiah 41:10)

Supplies

glue
paper
crayons
markers
scissors
stapler
staples
facial tissue,
  bathroom
  tissue, or cotton
  balls

Bible Story

For many years the Hebrew people lived happily in Egypt. One day a new pharaoh became the ruler. He did not like the Hebrew people. He made them slaves. He made them work very hard.

"The slaves will cut the stones and make the bricks to build my new cities," the pharaoh said.

One day a new baby was born into a Hebrew family. "The pharaoh does not like us. He will not be pleased that we have a baby boy. We must hide him to keep him safe," said his mother.

Soon the baby grew too big to hide. So, Jochebed made a basket for her son. She covered the outside with pitch so that it would float. She put soft blankets inside. Then Jochebed put her baby in the basket. She carried the basket to the river.

"Miriam, you must keep watch over your little brother," said Jochebed. So Miriam hid in the tall river grasses. Soon she heard voices coming down to the river. The pharaoh's daughter had come to the river to take a bath.

The princess saw the basket. She told her maid to pull the basket from the water and bring it to her. "Oh, what a beautiful baby! Some Hebrew mother has hidden her son here on the river. I will take this baby and protect him from my father," she exclaimed.

Miriam ran to the princess. "Shall I get someone to help you care for this baby?" she asked. When the princess nodded, Miriam ran as fast as she could to her own house.

"Mother, come quickly. The pharaoh's daughter has found our baby!" The two ran to the river.

The princess handed the baby to Jochebed. "Take care of this child for me. I will pay you." So Jochebed took her son home. There she loved him and took care of him. When he was older, she brought him to the princess at the palace. There the princess raised the boy as her own son. She named him Moses.

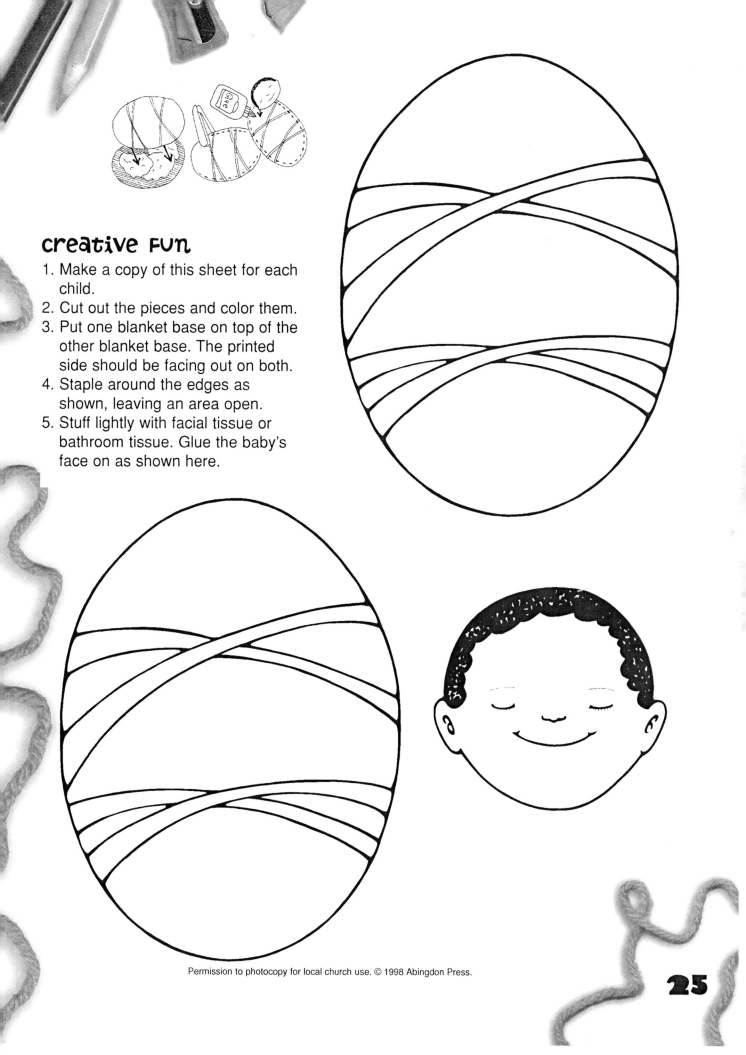

creative FUN

1. Make a copy of this sheet for each child.
2. Cut out the pieces and color them.
3. Put one blanket base on top of the other blanket base. The printed side should be facing out on both.
4. Staple around the edges as shown, leaving an area open.
5. Stuff lightly with facial tissue or bathroom tissue. Glue the baby's face on as shown here.

Permission to photocopy for local church use. © 1998 Abingdon Press.

A BURNING BUSH

The Bible
Exodus 2:11-16; 3:1-12

But even when I am afraid, I keep on trusting you.
(Psalm 56:3, CEV)

Supplies
glue
paper
crayons
markers
colored art
    tissue
water
small containers
paint brushes or
    cotton swabs

Bible Story

Moses grew up in the palace of the great pharaoh. But even though he lived the life of a royal prince, he never forgot that he was the son of a Hebrew slave.

One day Moses saw an overseer beating a slave. Moses became so angry that he hit the overseer. The overseer fell down dead. Now, Moses was frightened. What would he do? He would have to run away.

So Moses left Egypt and went to live in the country of Midian. Even though he was far away from Egypt, God still knew where he was. God had a plan for Moses.

One day while Moses was out caring for his father-in-law's sheep, he saw something strange. A bush on the hillside was burning, but it didn't burn up. Moses had to go and see this for himself.

Moses climbed the hillside to get a closer look. When he got near the bush, he heard a voice. "Come no closer. You are standing on holy ground. Take off your sandals." Moses did as the voice commanded.

"I am the God of your father and mother. The God of your Hebrew family long ago—Abraham, Isaac, and Jacob. I have heard my people crying out in Egypt. They want to be free. They need my help. I want you to bring my people out of Egypt to a land that I have planned for them."

"I cannot go back to Egypt," said Moses, thinking about what might happen. "Besides, I don't think I'm the right person for this job. I cannot speak well. You need someone else."

"Moses," said God, "I have chosen you! I will be with you. With me on your side, we cannot lose."

Creative Fun
1. Make a copy of the burning bush for each child.
2. Color the trunk, leaves, and branches of the bush.
3. Tear colored art tissue (yellow, red, orange) into small, thumb-sized pieces.

4. Make a solution of white glue and water. Pour the solution into a small container.
5. Have the children paint the pieces of tissue paper onto the burning bush using a cotton swab.

Permission to photocopy for local church use. © 2004 Abingdon Press.

LET MY PEOPLE GO!

the Bible

Exodus 6:7; 8-12

I will take you as my people, and I will be your God.

(Exodus 6:7)

supplies

paper
paper plate
crayons
markers
scissors
glue

Bible story

As Moses set out for Egypt, he came across his brother Aaron whom God had sent to be his helper. The two of them would go to the pharaoh together. They told the pharaoh, "God says, 'Let my people go!' "

The pharaoh looked at Moses. Then he looked at Aaron. "I don't know this god of yours. I won't listen to you! I won't let the people go. No, no, no! They cannot go!"

Not only did the pharaoh not let the people go, he made them work even harder. So God sent Moses back to the pharaoh.

"God says, 'Let my people go!' " said Moses and Aaron.

The pharaoh said, "I won't let the people go. No, no, no! They cannot go."

"If you don't let God's people go, terrible things are going to happen," Moses promised.

But the pharaoh would not change his mind, and God sent a plague of frogs. Frogs were everywhere—frogs in the beds, frogs in the fields, frogs in the food. Frogs, frogs, frogs.

The pharaoh said to Moses, "Make these frogs go away, and I will let your people go."

So God called back the frogs. When every last frog was gone, the pharaoh said, "I have changed my mind. I won't let the people go. No, no, no! They cannot go!"

Then God sent a plague of flies. Flies were everywhere. Flies in the beds, flies in the fields, flies in the food. Flies, flies, flies!

The pharaoh said to Moses, "Make the flies go away and I will let the people go." And when every last fly was gone, the pharaoh changed his mind. God sent more plagues. Every time the pharaoh promised to let the people go. Every time the pharaoh changed his mind. Finally God sent the most terrible plague of all. God sent the Angel of Death to every house in Egypt, but the angel passed over the homes of the Hebrew people.

Then the pharaoh said to Moses, "I will let your people go. Take them all and go, go, go!" And they did.

creative Fun

1. Make a copy of the frog eyes, tongue, and mouth for each child in the class.
2. Cut them out and color them.
3. Fold a thin, dinner-sized paper plate in half. Color the outside of the plate green. (If you can find a green paper plate, that will be faster.)
4. Fold the eyes in half. Glue the eyes to the outside top of the paper plate.
5. Color the mouth pattern red. Fold it in half. Put glue on the back side and place it inside the fold of the paper plate, matching the folds.
6. Attach the tongue on the fold at the back of the mouth.

Use the frog to tell the story of Moses and the Pharaoh.

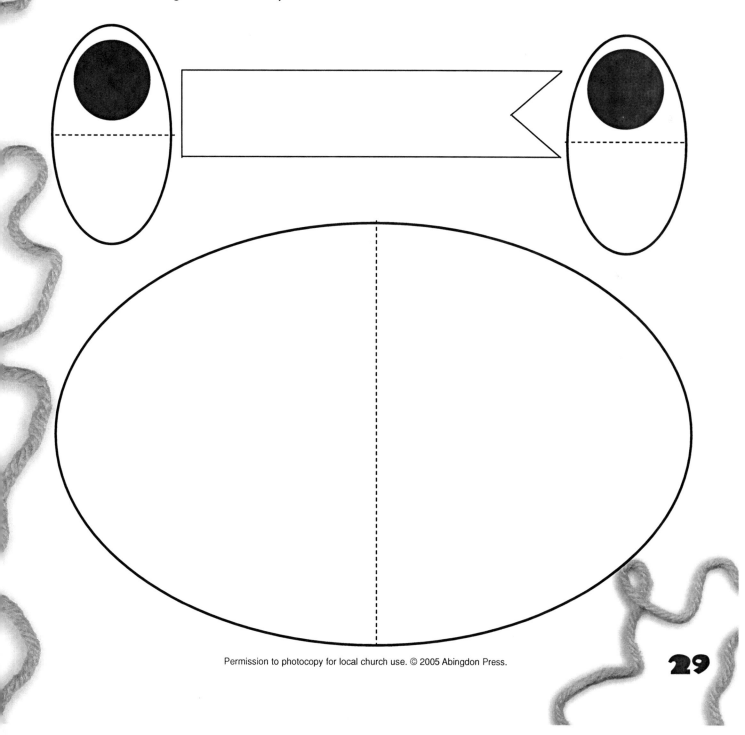

Permission to photocopy for local church use. © 2005 Abingdon Press.

IN THE WILDERNESS

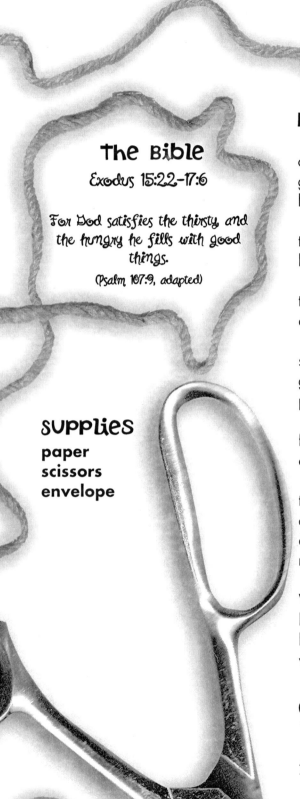

The Bible

Exodus 15:22–17:6

For God satisfies the thirsty, and the hungry he fills with good things.

(Psalm 107:9, adapted)

Supplies

paper
scissors
envelope

Bible Story

Now, with God's help, Moses led the Hebrew people out of slavery in Egypt. They started for the land that God was going to show them. No one knew exactly where this special land was located, so they had to follow where God led them.

First God led the people here. Then God led them there. Soon the food and water they had brought with them from Egypt had run out, and the people complained and complained.

God told Moses, "I will rain bread from heaven. Each day the people shall gather enough for that day only. But on the sixth day, they will gather enough for that day and the Sabbath."

Sure enough, the next morning there was a fine, flaky substance on the ground. The people gathered it and ground it into flour. From the flour they made bread. Still the people complained and complained. They had no meat.

So God sent quails to the camp. The quails were so tired from their long flight over the ocean that they were easy to catch. The people caught the quails and had meat for dinner.

Once again God led the people here. Then God led them there. Once again the people had no water to drink, and they complained and complained. God said to Moses, "I'm getting a little tired of these people and all their complaints. Strike that rock and water will come out of it. Let the people drink their fill."

So Moses struck the rock with his staff. Water trickled. Water flowed. Water gushed. Water poured. The people held their jars under the cool, sweet water. Now the people had bread. They had meat. They had water. Surely they would be content now. And they were—at least for now.

Creative Fun

1. Make two copies of the wilderness cards for each group of two children.
2. Cut the cards apart and place them face down on the table. Mix them up.
3. Play a game of concentration, turning up two cards at a time. If the two cards match, the player keeps the cards

and takes another turn. If the cards don't match, the cards are
turned over and play passes to the second player.

4. When all the cards are matched, the game is over. All of these items
   are things Moses and the Hebrew people would have encountered
   in the wilderness.

5. Store the cards in an envelope.

Permission to photocopy for local church use. © 1998 Abingdon Press.

TEN COMMANDMENTS

The Bible

Exodus 20:1-21

You shall have no other gods before me.

(Exodus 20:3)

Supplies

paper
crayons
markers
scissors
newspaper
cotton swabs
baby oil
shallow
  containers

Bible Story

For a long time the Hebrew people traveled in the wilderness. Finally, they came to the foot of a great mountain. God called Moses to come to the top of the mountain.

At the top of the mountain, God spoke to Moses. "Tell the people all that I have done. Tell them that I am their God. If they will obey me and keep my rules, they will be my special people. Bring them to me so that I can speak to them."

Moses went back down the mountain. He called the people together. They came to hear the words of God. But dark clouds and smoke covered the top of the mountain. Thunder rumbled. Lightning flashed. The ground shook. The people were afraid. They were afraid that the voice of God would hurt them.

So God called Moses back to the top of the mountain. "I don't want to frighten the people. Only you may climb this mountain and talk to me. From now on, you will tell the people what I say."

Moses listened to all that God had to say. Below, the people heard the thunder rumble. They saw the lightning flash. They felt the ground shake, but this time they weren't afraid. They knew God was talking to Moses.

When Moses came down from the mountain, he brought a list of rules that God had given to the people.

I will be your only God.

You will not make idols to worship.

You will not use my name in a bad way.

Remember the sabbath day. Keep it holy.

Honor your father and your mother.

Do not commit murder.

Be faithful in marriage.

Do not steal.

Do not tell lies.

Do not want what belongs to someone else.

"If you will obey these rules," Moses said, "then you will be God's special people."

creative fun

1. Make a copy of the stained glass window for each child.
2. Cut out the stained glass window. Place it on recycled newspaper.
3. Color the window with crayons or permanent markers.
4. Pour baby oil into shallow containers.
5. Dip the cotton swab in the baby oil and lightly rub it over the entire window.
6. Hang the picture in a sunny location. Can you find all the stories about Moses?

Permission to photocopy for local church use. © 2002 Abingdon Press.

A HOUSE FOR GOD

The Bible

Exodus 35-37

Worship the Lord with gladness.
(Psalm 100:2)

Supplies

paper
crayons
markers
scissors
cardboard
tape
glue

Bible Story

One day God said, "Moses, I have set aside the seventh day of every week as a holy day, a day of rest. I want the people to build a special place where they can come to worship me. Take up an offering from the people. Let them build me a Tabernacle."

So Moses called the people together and told them what God had said. "In this Tabernacle we will worship God. Wherever we go, we will take the Tabernacle with us. God wants each person to give what he or she can."

The people went back to their tents. They brought their offerings to Moses. They brought precious metals—gold and silver and bronze and copper. They brought cloth of blue and purple and scarlet. They brought animal skins—skins of goats, sheep, and cattle. They brought oil and incense. They brought acacia wood.

"No more! We have enough!" exclaimed Moses as the people brought their offerings. Then Moses said to Bezalel, "God has given you the skill to build the Tabernacle. You will be in charge, but everyone must help."

"I can sew," said one woman.

"I can weave," said another.

"I am a good builder," said a man.

"I can fashion metal," said another.

So, each person set to work. There were weavers and sewers and cloth dyers. There were metal workers and carpenters and tanners. Those who were not working on the Tabernacle, made food for those who were.

"We will make a special box," said Bezalel. "Inside we will put the tablets with the rules that God has given us. It will have a special place in our Tabernacle. We will carry it with us wherever we go. It will remind us that we are God's people."

Finally the Tabernacle was finished. The people came together. They had done all that God had asked them to do and more. They sang a song of praise to God in God's new house.

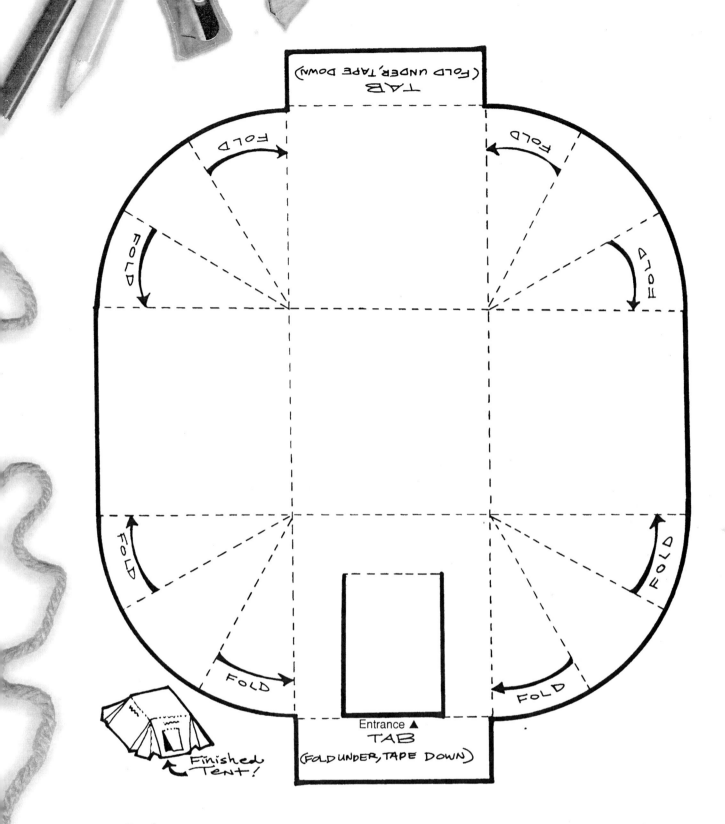

TAB
(FOLD UNDER, TAPE DOWN)

FOLD

FOLD

FOLD

FOLD

FOLD

FOLD

FOLD

FOLD

Entrance ▲
TAB
(FOLD UNDER, TAPE DOWN)

Finished Tent!

creative Fun

1. Make a copy of the Tabernacle for each child.
2. Cut out the Tabernacle and color it.
3. Cut the entrance to the Tabernacle. Fold it back.
4. Fold the sides as shown in the diagram.
5. Glue the Tabernacle to a piece of cardboard.

Permission to photocopy for local church use. © 2004 Abingdon Press.

DAVID

the Bible

1 Samuel 16:1–13

The LORD looks on the heart.
(1 Samuel 16:7)

Supplies

**glue
paper
cotton balls
  or cotton
  batting
cotton swabs
scissors
dark gray
  crayons or
  markers**

Bible Story

One day God said to Samuel, "Enough is enough! Saul no longer listens to me and follows my commands. I have chosen a new king. You must go to him and anoint him with oil."

"Wait a minute," said Samuel. "This is not going to make King Saul very happy. What will happen when he finds out where I'm going?"

"We'll keep it a secret. Tell the king that you're going to Bethlehem to have a special celebration. While you're there, you'll anoint the new king," said God.

Samuel wasn't convinced that he could get away without King Saul knowing, but he was obedient to God. Samuel quietly left the city and set out for Bethlehem.

The elders of the city saw him coming and met him at the gate. They were afraid because wherever Samuel went, trouble often followed. "Why are you here?" they asked.

"Don't be afraid," said Samuel. "I'm here to celebrate a special feast day at Jesse's home. You are all invited."

When Samuel got to Jesse's house, he told Jesse, "God has chosen a new king. He is one of your sons. Bring all of your sons here. God will tell me which one it is."

Jesse was very excited. One of his sons would be the new king. So, one by one, Jesse's sons came before Samuel. Each stood tall and straight and handsome. Samuel listened carefully for God to tell him which one to anoint, but so far no son was the right one.

"Don't be fooled by how a person looks," God said to Samuel. "I don't see as a person sees. I know what is on the inside of a person's heart."

Samuel asked Jesse if this was all of his sons. "I have one more, but he is the youngest and is out watching the sheep," said Jesse. Samuel told Jesse to send for him as well.

As soon as David stood before Samuel, God said, "This is the one I have chosen." Samuel took the special oil and poured it over David's head. From that day forward, the spirit of God filled David and was with him in all that he did. But it would still be years before David could take the throne.

creative FUN

1. Make a copy of the Bible verse tent card for each child in the group.
2. Color the face of the sheep dark gray.
3. Paint the body of the sheep with white glue using a cotton swab.
4. Press cotton balls or cotton batting over the body of the sheep.
5. Fold the tent card in half.
6. Place the card beside your bed to remind you that God doesn't judge by what we look like on the outside. God knows what's in our hearts.

David, who became the greatest king of all of Israel, was a shepherd boy.

The Lord looks on the heart.
(1 Samuel 16:7)

The LORD looks on the heart.
(1 Samuel 16:7)

Permission to photocopy for local church use. © 1998 Abingdon Press.

DAVID AND GOLIATH

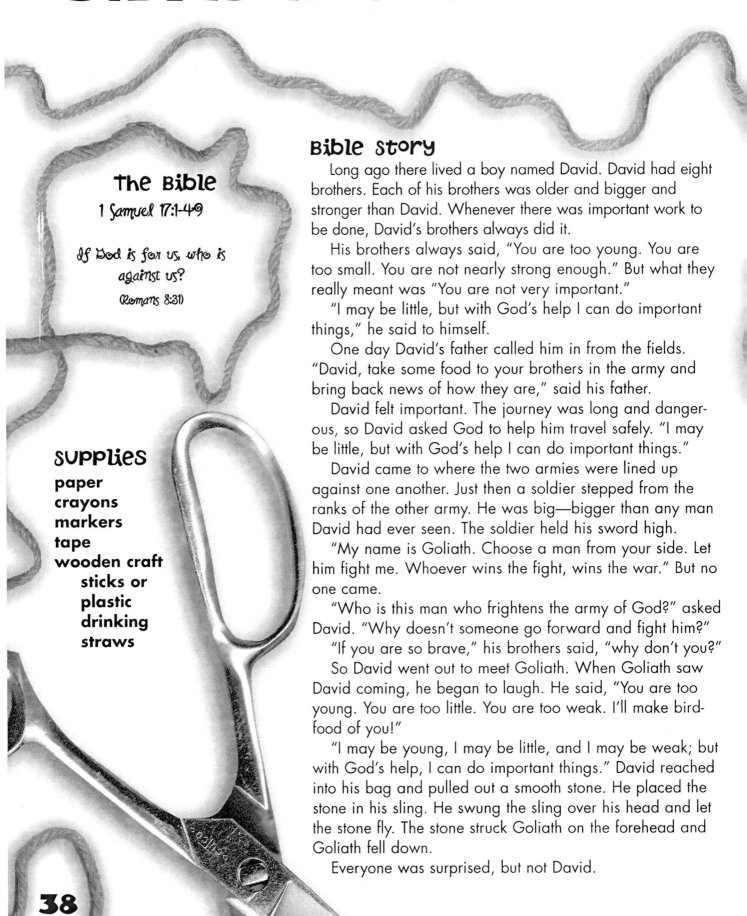

The Bible

1 Samuel 17:1-49

If God is for us, who is against us?

(Romans 8:31)

Supplies

paper
crayons
markers
tape
wooden craft sticks or plastic drinking straws

Bible Story

Long ago there lived a boy named David. David had eight brothers. Each of his brothers was older and bigger and stronger than David. Whenever there was important work to be done, David's brothers always did it.

His brothers always said, "You are too young. You are too small. You are not nearly strong enough." But what they really meant was "You are not very important."

"I may be little, but with God's help I can do important things," he said to himself.

One day David's father called him in from the fields. "David, take some food to your brothers in the army and bring back news of how they are," said his father.

David felt important. The journey was long and dangerous, so David asked God to help him travel safely. "I may be little, but with God's help I can do important things."

David came to where the two armies were lined up against one another. Just then a soldier stepped from the ranks of the other army. He was big—bigger than any man David had ever seen. The soldier held his sword high.

"My name is Goliath. Choose a man from your side. Let him fight me. Whoever wins the fight, wins the war." But no one came.

"Who is this man who frightens the army of God?" asked David. "Why doesn't someone go forward and fight him?"

"If you are so brave," his brothers said, "why don't you?"

So David went out to meet Goliath. When Goliath saw David coming, he began to laugh. He said, "You are too young. You are too little. You are too weak. I'll make bird-food of you!"

"I may be young, I may be little, and I may be weak; but with God's help, I can do important things." David reached into his bag and pulled out a smooth stone. He placed the stone in his sling. He swung the sling over his head and let the stone fly. The stone struck Goliath on the forehead and Goliath fell down.

Everyone was surprised, but not David.

creative fun

1. Make a copy of the story figures for each child.
2. Cut out the figures and color them.
3. Tape a wooden craft stick or plastic drinking straw to the back of each
   figure. Retell the story of David and Goliath using the figures.

Permission to photocopy for local church use. © 1997 Abingdon Press.

39

FOREVER FRIENDS

The Bible

1 Samuel 18:1-16; 19:1-7; 20:1-42

A friend loves at all times.
(Proverbs 17:17)

Supplies

paper
scissors
crayons
markers

Bible Story

David came to live at the palace of King Saul. He often played music for the King whenever the king was upset or angry. Everyone liked David. He was loyal to the king and a good leader. King Saul came to love David almost as much as he loved his own son Jonathan. In fact, Jonathan and David became best friends, almost like brothers.

The two young men promised to be friends forever. "No matter what happens, we will always be friends," they promised to one another.

One day David was playing the harp and singing for the king. King Saul began to think. The more he thought, the angrier he became. "What if the people decided to make David king instead of me? I wouldn't like that a bit." So King Saul picked up his spear and threw it at David.

Fortunately David was very quick and he ducked. The spear stuck in the wall above David's head.

Jonathan was worried about his father's feelings toward David. "For some reason, my father is angry with you. It is not safe for you at the palace. Go hide until I can find out what's going on."

David could not think of anything that he had done wrong. But he knew that King Saul was trying to kill him, so he hid. He and Jonathan invented a secret code. Jonathan wanted to protect his friend, but first Jonathan had to talk with his father.

King Saul promised not to harm David. But Jonathan knew better. Jonathan was sure that the palace was a dangerous place for David. He had to tell his friend to leave the country.

The next day Jonathan went out to the field with a servant. Jonathan shot an arrow into the air. "Run and fetch the arrow," Jonathan said to his servant. "Look, the arrow is beyond you. Hurry, do not linger."

The servant was confused. He was holding the arrow. But this was the secret signal that David and Jonathan had decided upon. Jonathan was telling David to leave and not return. Jonathan had to protect his friend David.

creative FUn

1. Make a copy of the friendship cards for each child.
2. Cut out the cards and color them.
3. Fold along the dotted line.
4. Write a special message on the inside and give the card to a friend.

Permission to photocopy for local church use. © 1997 Abingdon Press.

DAVID THE KING

The Bible
1 Samuel 24;
2 Samuel 2:1-7; 5:1-5

It is you who shall be shepherd of my people Israel.

(2 Samuel 5:2)

supplies
glue
paper
crayons
markers
scissors
cardboard
pencils
construction
  paper
tape
aluminum foil
(optional)

Bible Story

Because King Saul was so very jealous of David, David had to run away from the palace to be safe. But wherever David went, King Saul and his army were not far behind.

One night David slipped into the king's camp when everyone was fast asleep. David sneaked into King Saul's tent and took the king's spear and water jar. King Saul didn't know David had even been there.

The next morning, David stood on a hill near the king's camp. He called out in a loud voice, "Is this not your spear, O King? Is this not your water jar? If I had wanted to hurt you, last night I could have. Why don't you let me go my way in peace?"

King Saul was filled with great sadness. David could have killed him but had not. "I have made a mistake. Go in peace and never again will I try to hurt you," said the king. Saul and his armies left the camp and went back to their home.

Still there were many battles being fought with other countries. The armies fought long and hard. After one battle, David heard that King Saul and his son Jonathan had been killed. David was very sad. Jonathan had been his very best friend. But now the time that God had promised had come. David could finally become the king.

David's followers crowned him king. Now, with God's help, David would lead the people of Israel. He would bring all the tribes together into one great nation. This nation would be not just under David's rule but under God's rule as well.

Creative Fun

1. Make a copy of the shield pattern for each child.
2. Trace the shield onto cardboard.
3. Cut it out.
4. Create a design for a kingdom under God's rule.
5. Tape a folded strip of construction paper to the back as a handle.

Option: Instead of drawing the design, cut out the shapes from lightweight cardboard. Glue them onto the shield base.

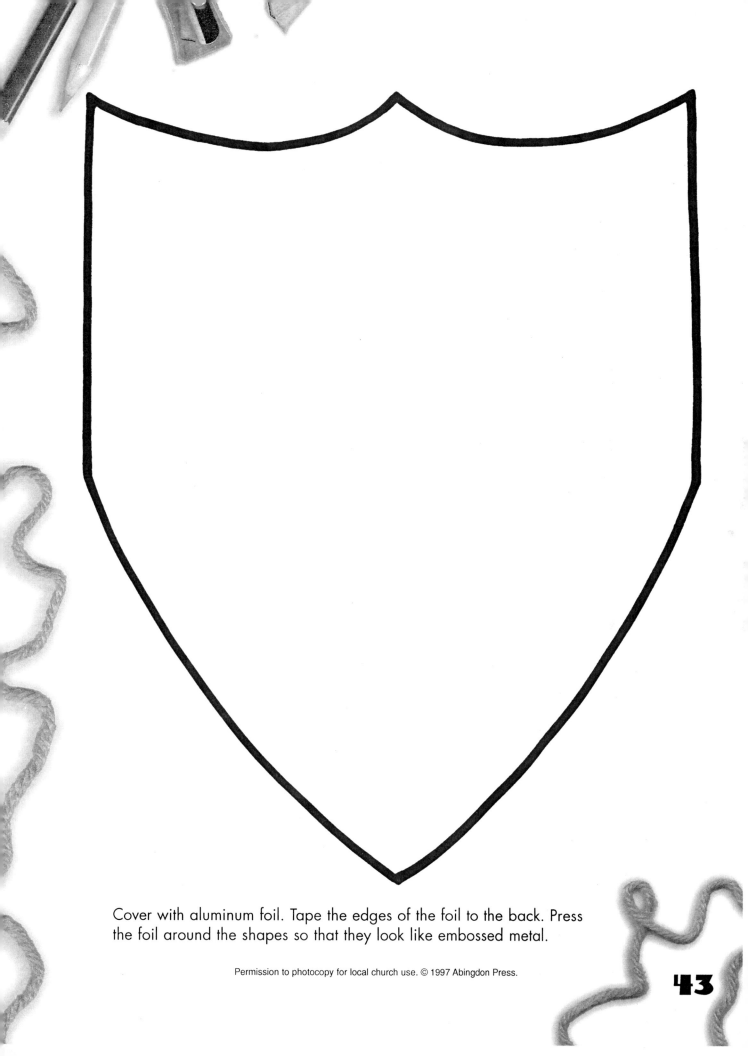

Cover with aluminum foil. Tape the edges of the foil to the back. Press the foil around the shapes so that they look like embossed metal.

Permission to photocopy for local church use. © 1997 Abingdon Press.

SOLOMON'S TEMPLE

The Bible

1 Kings 2:1-4; 3:1-15; 5:1-12; 6:1-37; 8:12-26, 54-61

Worship the LORD with gladness.

(Psalm 100:2)

Supplies

paper
scissors
envelope

Bible Story

While David was king, the Hebrew people became a strong and powerful nation. One day when David was an old man, he called his youngest son, Solomon, to him. There were many things David wanted to tell his son before he died.

"Being a king is not easy," David said to his son. "When bad things happen, and they will, be strong. Ask God to help you. Obey all of God's laws and commandments. As long as the people are faithful, God will be with us."

One night after Solomon became king, God said to him in a dream, "If I were to give you any gift, what would it be?"

Solomon thought and thought. He could ask for riches, but he already had wealth. He could ask for a great kingdom, but his father had already left that to him. He could ask for death to his enemies, but that was not what he wanted. "I am young and do not know how to rule the people wisely. Give me the wisdom I need to rule your people."

God was pleased with Solomon. "I will make you the wisest king who ever lived. I will also give you great wealth and honor if you obey me and keep my laws just as your father did."

At last God's people were at peace. Solomon decided to build a great house for God. For seven years the people worked on the Temple. When it was finally finished, no one had ever seen such a wondrous place. The inside walls were covered in gold. Even the floors were gold.

Solomon called the leaders of the people together. He made an offering to God and prayed, "You, God, have placed the sun in the sky, and yet you have chosen to live in clouds and darkness. Now I have built a beautiful house for you to live in forever."

Creative Fun

1. For each pair of children, make two copies of the items that went into Solomon's Temple.
2. Cut the cards apart. Turn them face down.
3. Mix them up. Then one at a time, each player will try to find matches for the various items.

Permission to photocopy for local church use. © 2000 Abingdon Press.

RAVENS FOR ELIJAH

The Bible
1 Kings 17:1-24

God satisfies the thirsty, and the hungry he fills with good things.
(Psalm 107:9, adapted)

Supplies
glue
paper
crayons
markers
scissors
tape

Bible Story

Ahab was the king of all of Israel, but Ahab was not a very good king. He did wicked things. He did not follow God's laws. He did not live as God wanted him to live.

One day God decided it was time for Ahab to change his ways. God spoke to a man named Elijah. Elijah was a prophet. He told the people what God wanted them to do.

"You must tell King Ahab that he is such a wicked king that I am going to punish the whole land and everyone in it. I will bring a terrible drought. There will be no rain for weeks and weeks. As soon as you tell the king this, you must go and hide. Ahab is sure to be very angry with you, but I will take care of you."

Elijah went to see the king. He told King Ahab what a wicked king he had been. He told King Ahab that God was going to punish not only the king but the entire land for King Ahab's wickedness. Then Elijah went to hide because, just as God had predicted, King Ahab was very angry.

Elijah went to a small cave that God had told him about. A brook ran beside the cave so that Elijah could have water, and every morning and every evening God sent ravens to bring food to Elijah.

Elijah was sad for the people because the drought went on for two years. But God cared for Elijah and kept him safe.

Creative Fun

1. Make a copy of the raven for each child.
2. Color the bird and cut out the pieces.
3. Assemble the bird by gluing or taping the wings into place.
4. Glue the raven's beak in place.
5. Tape the two flaps together under the bird.
6. Slip your hand into that space.
7. Pretend you are the raven bringing food to Elijah.

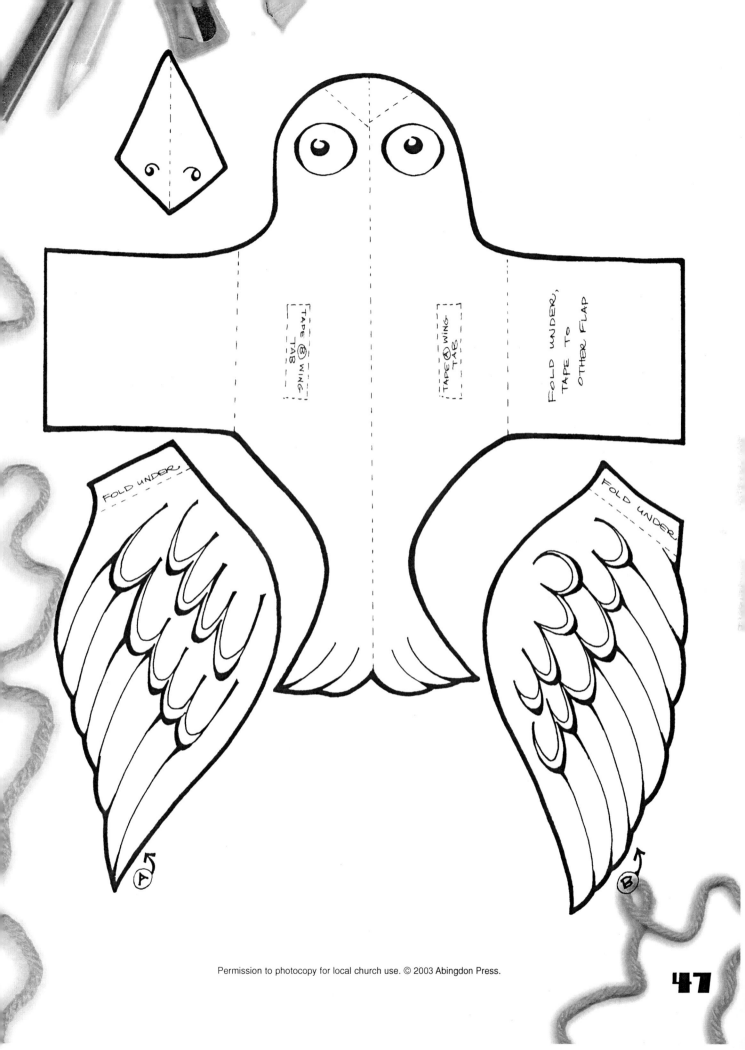

TAPE Ⓑ WING TAB

TAPE Ⓐ WING TAB

FOLD UNDER, TAPE TO OTHER FLAP

FOLD UNDER

FOLD UNDER

Ⓐ

Ⓑ

Permission to photocopy for local church use. © 2003 Abingdon Press.

THE LIONS' DEN

The Bible

Daniel 6

The name of the LORD is to be praised.

(Psalm 113:3)

Supplies

glue
paper
scissors
crayons
markers
cardboard
    squares
tape
wooden craft
    stick or folded
    construction
    paper

Creative Fun

1. Make a copy of the lion puppet for each child.
2. Color the puppet pieces.
3. Cut the pieces out and assemble as shown. Add small bits of cardboard to the back of each piece before gluing it to the base. This makes the puppet three dimensional.
4. Attach a craft stick or folded construction paper to the back of the puppet for a handle. Use the puppet in the story.

Bible Story

In a land so far away,
There lived a man who liked to pray.
He prayed to God three times a day.
Roar! Roar! Roar! *(Use the puppets to roar.)*

Some jealous men dreamed up a plan.
A new law was sent throughout the land,
Decreeing prayers to God were banned.
Roar! Roar! Roar! *(Use the puppets to roar.)*

But Daniel chose to do what's right,
And in his room within plain sight,
He prayed to God both day and night.
Roar! Roar! Roar! *(Use the puppets to roar.)*

Daniel was the king's good friend,
but still he was put into the den
Because of those most jealous men.
Roar! Roar! Roar! *(Use the puppets to roar.)*

With lions Daniel spent the night.
The king rushed down at morning's light
To find that Daniel was all right.
Roar! Roar! Roar! *(Use the puppets to roar.)*

So the king pronounced a *new* decree.
"The God of Daniel, as you see,
the One True God will always be."
Roar! Roar! Roar! *(Use the puppets to roar.)*

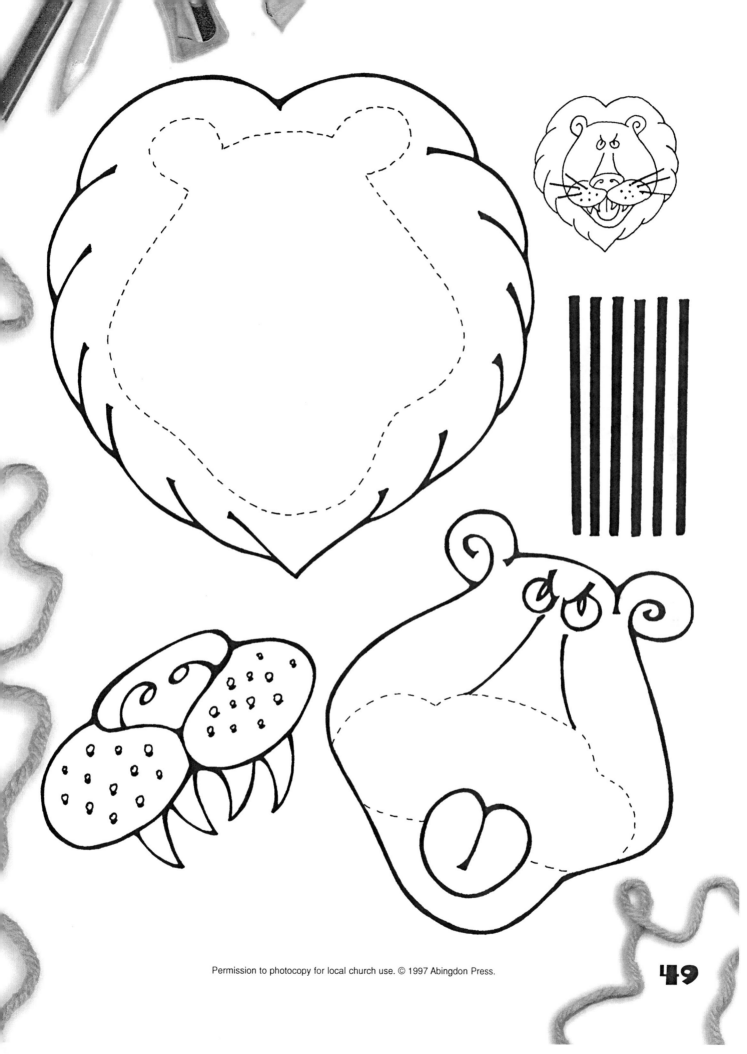

Permission to photocopy for local church use. © 1997 Abingdon Press.

49

QUEEN ESTHER

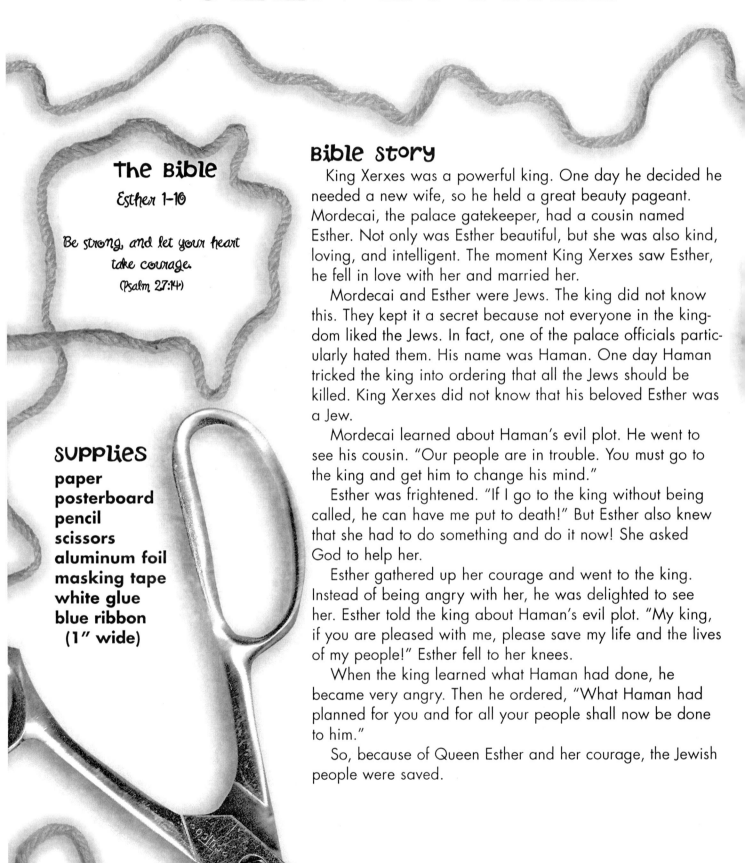

The Bible

Esther 1-10

Be strong, and let your heart
take courage.
(Psalm 27:14)

Supplies

**paper
posterboard
pencil
scissors
aluminum foil
masking tape
white glue
blue ribbon
(1" wide)**

Bible Story

King Xerxes was a powerful king. One day he decided he needed a new wife, so he held a great beauty pageant. Mordecai, the palace gatekeeper, had a cousin named Esther. Not only was Esther beautiful, but she was also kind, loving, and intelligent. The moment King Xerxes saw Esther, he fell in love with her and married her.

Mordecai and Esther were Jews. The king did not know this. They kept it a secret because not everyone in the kingdom liked the Jews. In fact, one of the palace officials particularly hated them. His name was Haman. One day Haman tricked the king into ordering that all the Jews should be killed. King Xerxes did not know that his beloved Esther was a Jew.

Mordecai learned about Haman's evil plot. He went to see his cousin. "Our people are in trouble. You must go to the king and get him to change his mind."

Esther was frightened. "If I go to the king without being called, he can have me put to death!" But Esther also knew that she had to do something and do it now! She asked God to help her.

Esther gathered up her courage and went to the king. Instead of being angry with her, he was delighted to see her. Esther told the king about Haman's evil plot. "My king, if you are pleased with me, please save my life and the lives of my people!" Esther fell to her knees.

When the king learned what Haman had done, he became very angry. Then he ordered, "What Haman had planned for you and for all your people shall now be done to him."

So, because of Queen Esther and her courage, the Jewish people were saved.

creative fun

1. Make a copy of the "Hero for God" medal for each child in your class.
2. Cut out the larger circle and use it as a pattern to cut one circle from posterboard.
3. Cover the circle with aluminum foil.
4. Tape the foil to the back of the circle.
5. Glue the "Hero for God" circle in the center of that circle.
6. Cut a strip of blue ribbon about twelve inches long.
7. Fold the ribbon in half.
8. Tape the folded edge of the ribbon to the back of the posterboard circle.

Esther had courage and stood up for her people. She was a "Hero for God." Present this medal to someone you think is a true "Hero for God." Make more than one medal if you have several people you think are heroes.

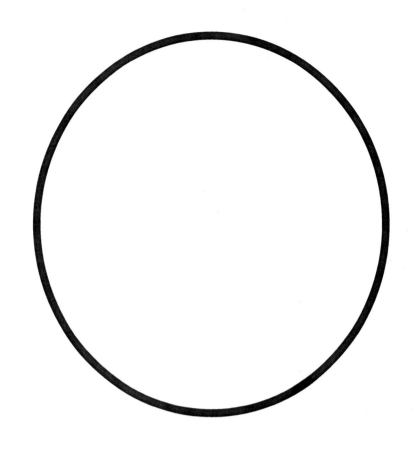

Permission to photocopy for local church use. © 2005 Abingdon Press.

NEHEMIAH'S WALL

The Bible

Nehemiah 2-6

We depend on you, LORD, to help and protect us.
(Psalm 33:20, CEV)

Supplies

paper
scissors
crayons
markers
construction
    paper
penny for each
    team

Bible Story

You've got to swing a mighty mallet *(Pretend to swing mallet)*
You've got to push and pull the saw *(Pretend to saw)*
You've got to stack the stones together *(Pound fists together)*
If you're going to build a wall. *(Touch floor and reach up)*

A long, long time ago in the country of God's people, a terrible army swept across the land. This army defeated every country in its path. As the army went, it also carried many people far, far away from their homeland. But as with most terrible armies, the time came when even they were defeated. God's people could go back to their homeland. **(Refrain)**

Nehemiah worked for the king. He heard the stories the people told about how they went back to Jerusalem to find the city in ruins. Everything was torn down, even the walls around the city. Nehemiah wanted to do something. **(Refrain)**

Nehemiah asked the king if he could go back to Jerusalem and help the people rebuild the wall around the city. Then the people there would be safe. The king agreed and even sent supplies to help. **(Refrain)**

Nehemiah told the people, "People, before we can do anything else, we must rebuild the walls. Each of us must do our part. We must ask God to help us. We can work together with God's help." **(Refrain)**

Some people didn't want the walls rebuilt. Soldiers would throw spears or shoot arrows at the workers. Some people didn't think that Nehemiah could rebuild the walls. They made fun of those who were working. **(Refrain)**

So Nehemiah assigned some people to be guards to protect those who were working. Those who didn't work on the walls made food and brought water to those who did. Brick by brick and stone by stone, the wall grew taller and stronger. In fifty-two days the wall was finished. When the final gate was hung in place, Nehemiah called the people together for a celebration.

"Thank you, God, for your help. Because of you, we could do this important thing," Nehemiah prayed.

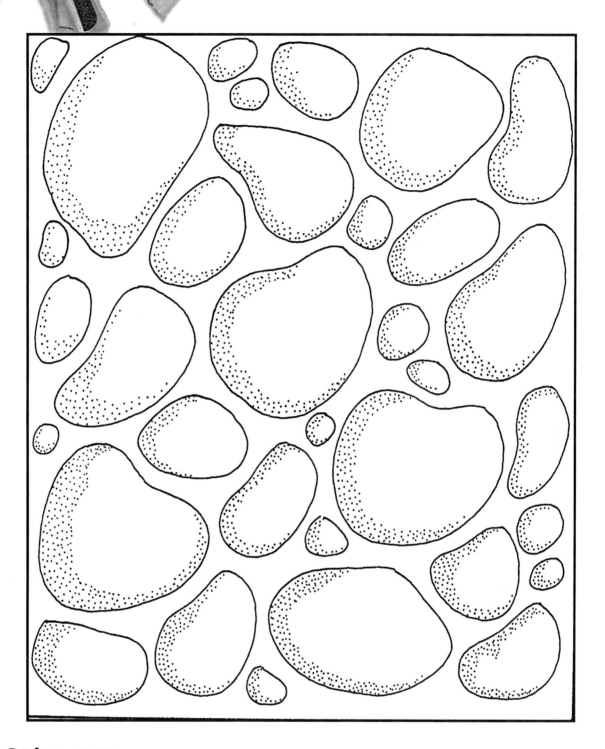

creative fun

1. Make a copy of the wall for each child.
2. Cut out the wall. Color it.
3. Divide the children into pairs. Give each pair a penny.
4. Tear construction paper into thirty-four thumb-sized bits. These will be the stones for the wall.
5. In turn each player will toss the penny. If the penny lands on heads, that player covers two stones with construction paper. If the penny lands on tails, the player covers one stone with a piece of construction paper. See who can build a wall the fastest.

Permission to photocopy for local church use. © 1998 Abingdon Press.

JONAH AND THE FISH

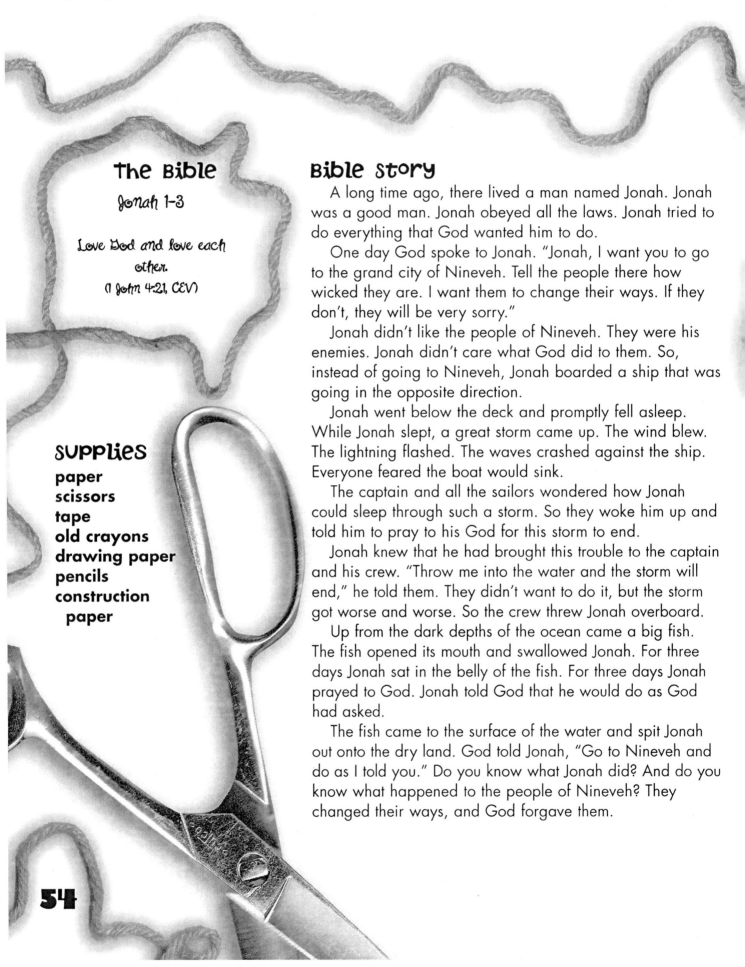

The Bible

Jonah 1-3

Love God and love each other.
(1 John 4:21, CEV)

Supplies

paper
scissors
tape
old crayons
drawing paper
pencils
construction
  paper

Bible Story

A long time ago, there lived a man named Jonah. Jonah was a good man. Jonah obeyed all the laws. Jonah tried to do everything that God wanted him to do.

One day God spoke to Jonah. "Jonah, I want you to go to the grand city of Nineveh. Tell the people there how wicked they are. I want them to change their ways. If they don't, they will be very sorry."

Jonah didn't like the people of Nineveh. They were his enemies. Jonah didn't care what God did to them. So, instead of going to Nineveh, Jonah boarded a ship that was going in the opposite direction.

Jonah went below the deck and promptly fell asleep. While Jonah slept, a great storm came up. The wind blew. The lightning flashed. The waves crashed against the ship. Everyone feared the boat would sink.

The captain and all the sailors wondered how Jonah could sleep through such a storm. So they woke him up and told him to pray to his God for this storm to end.

Jonah knew that he had brought this trouble to the captain and his crew. "Throw me into the water and the storm will end," he told them. They didn't want to do it, but the storm got worse and worse. So the crew threw Jonah overboard.

Up from the dark depths of the ocean came a big fish. The fish opened its mouth and swallowed Jonah. For three days Jonah sat in the belly of the fish. For three days Jonah prayed to God. Jonah told God that he would do as God had asked.

The fish came to the surface of the water and spit Jonah out onto the dry land. God told Jonah, "Go to Nineveh and do as I told you." Do you know what Jonah did? And do you know what happened to the people of Nineveh? They changed their ways, and God forgave them.

creative Fun

1. Make a copy of Jonah and the fish for each child.
2. Cut out the fish. Trace the fish onto a piece of construction paper. Cut it out.
3. Cut out the figure of Jonah. Trace Jonah onto a piece of construction paper. Cut it out.
4. Put a loop of tape on the back of the construction paper fish. Lightly tape it to the table.
5. Place a piece of drawing paper over the fish. Tape down lightly.
6. Remove the paper from a broken crayon and rub over the drawing paper. Watch the fish appear on the paper.
7. Change colors of crayons. Lift the top sheet of paper. Put a loop of tape on the back of the figure of Jonah. Position Jonah inside the outline of the construction paper fish.
8. Rub the crayon over the drawing once again. Watch Jonah appear inside the fish.

Permission to photocopy for local church use. © 2003 Abingdon Press.

THE LOST SCROLLS

The Bible

2 Kings 22:1-23:3

Love the LORD your God and obey all the laws and teachings. (Deuteronomy 11:22, CEV)

Supplies

paper
black
    construction
    paper
tape
straight pins or
    map push
    pins

Bible Story

Once there was a young boy whose name was Josiah. He was eight years old, and he was the new king of Judah. Unlike the kings before him, Josiah was faithful to God and asked God to help him be the very best king he could be.

As Josiah grew, he saw that the people around him were not living as God had told them to. "How can they know what God requires if they have no place to worship God?" Josiah thought to himself. So Josiah decided to make the Temple of Jerusalem as beautiful as it had been many years before.

Josiah put workmen in charge of removing all the rubble that had filled the Temple. But one day one of the workmen found something special—a large parchment scroll hidden away in a big clay jar.

The priest brought the scroll to Josiah who unrolled it and began to read. As he read he became quite troubled. His brow crinkled. His beard twitched. His eyes blinked, and he scratched his chin.

"My people have not seen this scroll for many years. Some of the rules that are written here have never been heard by the people. My people are being unfaithful to God, and they don't even know it," said Josiah.

Josiah took the scroll to the prophetess Huldah. She would know what to do with this scroll. Carefully Huldah unrolled the scroll and began to read. As she read, she became quite troubled. Her brow crinkled. Her eyes blinked. Her nose twitched. She scratched her chin.

"These are truly the words of God," Huldah said. "This is the lost Book of the Law of Moses. Truly our people have not been following God's rules. But God will give them another chance."

Josiah called all the people together. He began to read the words of the long-lost law. The people listened carefully. They became quite troubled. Their brows crinkled. Their ears twitched. Their eyes blinked. They scratched their heads. Then they all promised to be faithful to God. They would live by God's commandments.

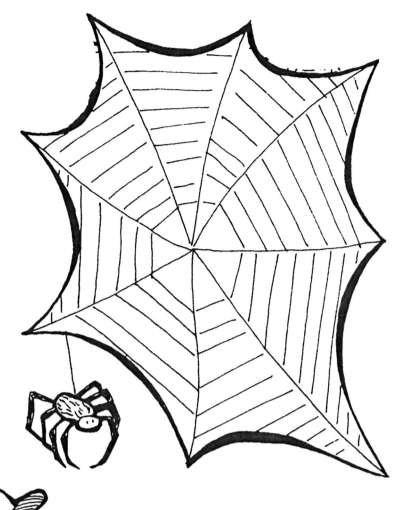

creative fun

1. Make a copy of this picture for each child in the class.
2. Have the children place the picture over a sheet of black construction paper.
3. Tape the top and bottom so that the top picture does not move.
4. Using a straight pin or map push pin, poke holes along each of the lines of the picture.
5. When you have finished, remove the top sheet and hold the construction paper up to the light.

What did the workmen find as they were repairing the Temple?

Permission to photocopy for local church use. © 1999 Abingdon Press.

PEACEFUL KINGDOM

The Bible
Isaiah 9:1-7; 11:1-9

The people who walked in darkness have seen a great light.
(Isaiah 9:2)

Supplies
paper
crayons
markers
scissors
ribbon or yarn
white glue

Bible Story

Long ago in the country of Judah lived a man named Isaiah. Isaiah was a prophet. God spoke to Isaiah. Isaiah then told the people what God had said. Isaiah was God's messenger.

At the time Isaiah lived, life was not good for the Hebrew people. The countries that surrounded them were fighting with one another. The rich farmers took land away from the poor farmers. The powerful people mistreated the poor people. The people were sad. They cried out to God, "Please send someone to save us!"

God heard the people and sent a message to them through Isaiah. "A child will be born for you. He will be the leader for God's people. He will be called the Savior and the Prince of Peace. He will be the Son of God. He will be a bright light for those people who are now living in darkness. He will show the people what God is like. He will save them.

"This new ruler will come from the family of King David. The spirit of God will be with him and give him great understanding, wisdom, and insight. He will be honest and fair. It will be a time of great peace.

"Leopards will lie down with young goats, and wolves will rest with lambs. Calves and lions will eat together and be cared for by little children. Cows and bears will share the same pasture; their young will rest side by side. Lions and oxen will both eat straw. The land will be filled with people who know and honor the Lord."

How happy the people were to hear Isaiah's words! The people thought, "Life may be bad now, but it will get better. God loves us and cares for us."

But the people still had to wait—until the time was right.

creative fun

1. Make a copy of the Bible bookmark for each child in the group.
2. Have the children color the bookmark and the gift "dangler."
3. Cut a piece of yarn or ribbon about ten inches long.
4. Fold the bookmark in half on the dotted line.
5. Spread white glue on one of the inside panels of the bookmark.
6. Lay one end of the yarn in the center of the panel with the glue.
7. Close the bookmark, sandwiching the yarn between the two halves. Press firmly.
8. Fold the gift "dangler" in half on the dotted lines.
9. Put glue on one of the inside panels.
10. Sandwich the remaining end of the yarn between the two sides of the "dangler."

The bookmark will fit into the Bible. The "dangler" will hang outside the Bible.

Permission to photocopy for local church use. © 1997 Abingdon Press.

GOOD NEWS, MARY

The Bible

Luke 1:26-38

For a child has been born for us.
(Isaiah 9:6)

Supplies
white glue
paper
scissors
yarn

Bible Story

Mary lived with her parents in the little town of Nazareth. Every day she helped her mother with the chores. She swept the dirt floors. She mended the family clothing. She mixed the flour and yeast for the bread.

As Mary worked, she daydreamed about the time when she would marry Joseph, the carpenter of the village. She smiled as she thought about it. Suddenly a bright light filled the dark room. Right in front of Mary was an angel.

"Greetings, favored one," said the angel. "The Lord is with you."

Mary was surprised. She had never met an angel before. Mary was also frightened. *What could the angel want with me?* she wondered. Angels were not an everyday happening.

"Don't be afraid, Mary. God is very pleased with you," said the angel. "You will have a baby boy. You will name him Jesus. He will grow up to be a very important person. Your baby is the Savior that everyone has been waiting for."

Mary was very surprised by the news. "How can this be?" she asked. "Joseph and I are not married."

"Nothing is too hard for God," answered the angel. "Your child will be called the Son of God. God's spirit will come to you."

Mary loved God very much. She could hardly believe that she was the one whom God had chosen. "Let it be as you say," said Mary. "I am God's servant." And the angel left.

Creative Fun
1. Make a copy of the angel for each child.
2. Cut a twelve-inch length of yarn for each angel ornament.
3. Cut out the angel shapes.
4. Spread glue on one of the angel bodies (but not the wings).
5. Fold the length of yarn in half, placing the ends on the glue-covered angel's chest. Make sure the loop extends beyond the angel's head.

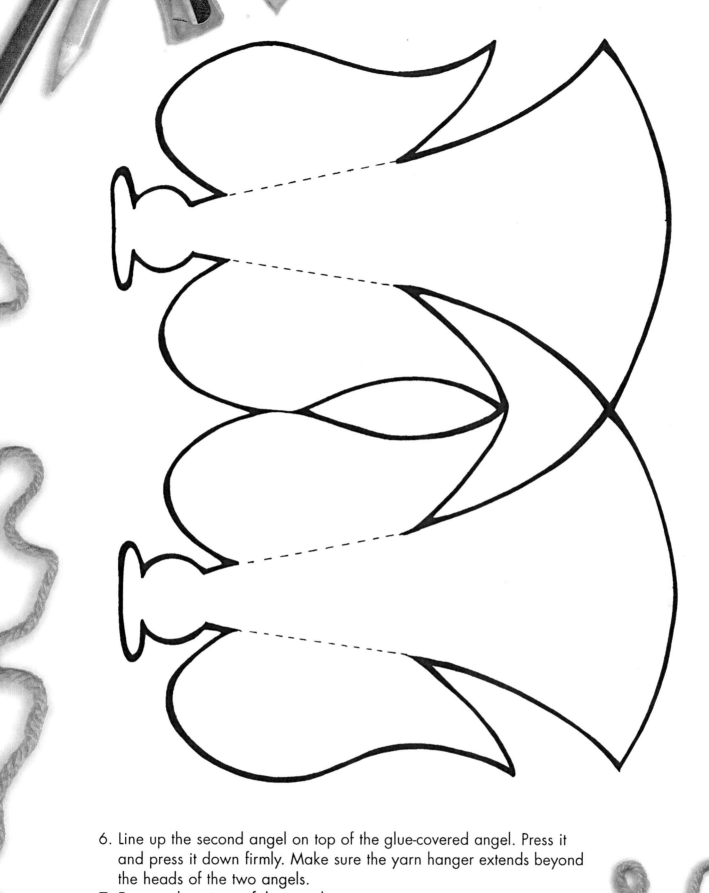

6. Line up the second angel on top of the glue-covered angel. Press it and press it down firmly. Make sure the yarn hanger extends beyond the heads of the two angels.
7. Fan out the wings of the angel.

Permission to photocopy for local church use. © 2004 Abingdon Press.

JESUS IS BORN

The Bible
Luke 2:1-7

She gave birth to her firstborn son and wrapped him in bands of cloth and laid him in a manger.
(Luke 2:7)

Supplies
shoebox
paper
scissors
crayons
markers
construction
  paper
tape
white glue

Bible Story

(Make trumpet sounds.) Give ear! Give ear! By order of the Emperor Augustus, all men will go to their home town to be registered. *(Make trumpet sounds.)*

So Joseph went from Nazareth in Galilee to Judea, to the city of David called Bethlehem, because he was from the family of David. And he took with him Mary, who was expecting a child.

(Pat legs.) Up the hills and down the hills the little donkey walked. The sun was going down. Soon it would be night. Mary was tired. Joseph was tired, and the little donkey was even more tired.

When the three came to Bethlehem, there was quite a crowd. *(Make crowd sounds.)* The streets were filled with travelers. In fact, the city was so crowded that there was no place to stay.

Joseph went from house to house. No one had any room. There was not an inch of floor space to be found. Finally he came to an inn. *(Knock on door.)* The innkeeper opened the door.

"We have no room tonight!" the innkeeper grumbled. Then he saw Mary. He felt sorry for them. "Wait, I have no room inside the inn, but I do have a stable. It's where the travelers keep their animals. You may sleep there tonight if you'd like," he said.

The innkeeper led Joseph and Mary and the tired little donkey to the small stable. It wasn't much, but there would be a roof over them tonight. And the animals would keep them company. *(Make animal sounds.)*

That night, in a small stable out behind the inn, Mary gave birth to baby Jesus. *(Make baby cries.)* She wrapped him in bands of cloth and laid him in the manger because there was no room in the inn.

Creative Fun
1. Make a copy of the Nativity figures for each child.
2. Color the figures and cut them out.

3. Cut a shoe box in half. (Each shoebox will make two stables.)
4. Cover the box with brown construction paper. Turn the box on its side.
5. Place the figures in the "stable."

Permission to photocopy for local church use. © 1998 Abingdon Press.

THE SHEPHERDS

The Bible
Luke 2:8-20

To you is born this day in the city of David a Savior, who is the Messiah, the Lord.

(Luke 2:11)

Supplies
paper
scissors
crayons
markers
tape
yarn or ribbon

Bible Story

It was a dark and windy night.
The stars were shining big and bright.
But in the air there was a chill
For the sheep and shepherds on that hill.

Soon every creature settled down.
From shepherd or sheep there wasn't a sound.
When all of a sudden from way up high,
A bright light filled the night-time sky.

And from the light the shepherd could hear,
"We bring you good news, so please don't fear.
We tell of a special babe that's been born
In the city of Bethlehem on this very morn."

"We bring you good news and news of great joy!
That will come to you with the birth of this boy.
He is the Savior, the King of all kings.
He is the one for whom we now sing."

"And should you go looking, you'll find him asleep
In a stable where animals a faithful watch keep."
And then with the one that had told the strange story,
There appeared many more, singing, "Glory, all glory!"

"Peace to all people, all people of earth.
Our world will find peace because of this birth."
Then the shepherds turned to each other in awe.
They were not quite sure what they heard and they saw.

"Let's see this great thing of which we've been told—
The babe that fulfills the Scriptures of old."
And they found the sweet child as the angels had said,
Asleep in a stable, a manger his bed.

And in that stable so safe and so warm,
God's only son, the Christ child was born.
Today we sing carols that tell of the birth,
"Peace to all people, all people of earth."

Hark, the Herald Angel Sings!

creative fun

1. Make a copy of the angel ornament for each child.
2. Color the ornament with crayons or markers.
3. Cut out the angel on the dark solid lines. (*Cut down the arms of the angel to the place where the arms meet the angel's gown. This frees the top half of the angel's body.*)
4. Cut a slit from the inside edge of the wing to the circle with the *B* in it.
5. Cut a second slit from the outside of the wing to the circle with the *A* in it.
6. Roll the angel into a cone-shape, slipping the slit marked *A* into the slit marked *B*. (*The angel's hands will form the top of the cone.*)
7. Punch a hole where indicated by the angel's hands. Tie a piece of yarn through the hole.

Permission to photocopy for local church use. © 2003 Abingdon Press.

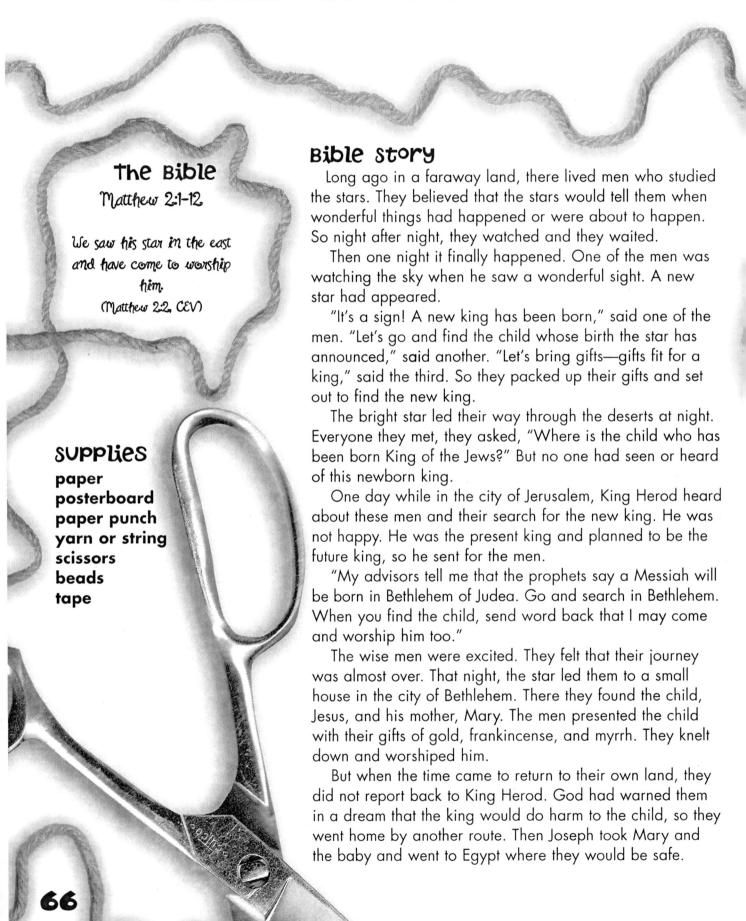

THE WISE MEN

the Bible

Matthew 2:1-12

We saw his star in the east and have come to worship him.

(Matthew 2:2, CEV)

supplies

**paper
posterboard
paper punch
yarn or string
scissors
beads
tape**

Bible story

Long ago in a faraway land, there lived men who studied the stars. They believed that the stars would tell them when wonderful things had happened or were about to happen. So night after night, they watched and they waited.

Then one night it finally happened. One of the men was watching the sky when he saw a wonderful sight. A new star had appeared.

"It's a sign! A new king has been born," said one of the men. "Let's go and find the child whose birth the star has announced," said another. "Let's bring gifts—gifts fit for a king," said the third. So they packed up their gifts and set out to find the new king.

The bright star led their way through the deserts at night. Everyone they met, they asked, "Where is the child who has been born King of the Jews?" But no one had seen or heard of this newborn king.

One day while in the city of Jerusalem, King Herod heard about these men and their search for the new king. He was not happy. He was the present king and planned to be the future king, so he sent for the men.

"My advisors tell me that the prophets say a Messiah will be born in Bethlehem of Judea. Go and search in Bethlehem. When you find the child, send word back that I may come and worship him too."

The wise men were excited. They felt that their journey was almost over. That night, the star led them to a small house in the city of Bethlehem. There they found the child, Jesus, and his mother, Mary. The men presented the child with their gifts of gold, frankincense, and myrrh. They knelt down and worshiped him.

But when the time came to return to their own land, they did not report back to King Herod. God had warned them in a dream that the king would do harm to the child, so they went home by another route. Then Joseph took Mary and the baby and went to Egypt where they would be safe.

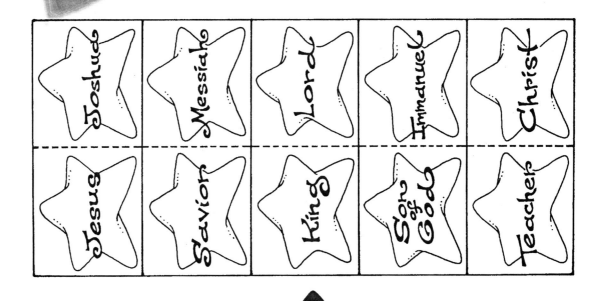

creative Fun

1. Make a copy of the name mobile for each child.
2. Use the star as a pattern to cut a second star from posterboard.
3. Punch holes as shown on the star.
4. Cut yarn or string into twelve-inch lengths. You will need eleven pieces for each mobile.
5. Attach a string to each of the holes on the points of the star.
6. Tie a bead onto the end of the center piece of yarn.
7. Thread the yarn with the bead up through the center hole.
8. Attach one of the names for Jesus to each of the strings with tape. Hang the mobile.

Permission to photocopy for local church use. © 1997 Abingdon Press.

JESUS IN THE TEMPLE

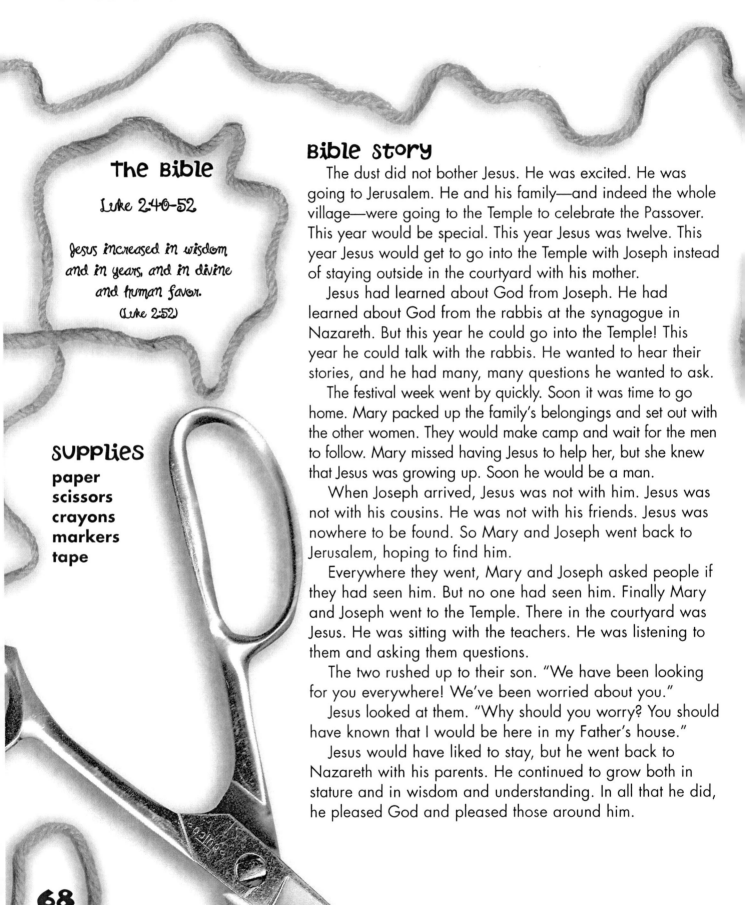

the Bible

Luke 2:40-52

Jesus increased in wisdom and in years, and in divine and human favor.
(Luke 2:52)

supplies

paper
scissors
crayons
markers
tape

Bible story

The dust did not bother Jesus. He was excited. He was going to Jerusalem. He and his family—and indeed the whole village—were going to the Temple to celebrate the Passover. This year would be special. This year Jesus was twelve. This year Jesus would get to go into the Temple with Joseph instead of staying outside in the courtyard with his mother.

Jesus had learned about God from Joseph. He had learned about God from the rabbis at the synagogue in Nazareth. But this year he could go into the Temple! This year he could talk with the rabbis. He wanted to hear their stories, and he had many, many questions he wanted to ask.

The festival week went by quickly. Soon it was time to go home. Mary packed up the family's belongings and set out with the other women. They would make camp and wait for the men to follow. Mary missed having Jesus to help her, but she knew that Jesus was growing up. Soon he would be a man.

When Joseph arrived, Jesus was not with him. Jesus was not with his cousins. He was not with his friends. Jesus was nowhere to be found. So Mary and Joseph went back to Jerusalem, hoping to find him.

Everywhere they went, Mary and Joseph asked people if they had seen him. But no one had seen him. Finally Mary and Joseph went to the Temple. There in the courtyard was Jesus. He was sitting with the teachers. He was listening to them and asking them questions.

The two rushed up to their son. "We have been looking for you everywhere! We've been worried about you."

Jesus looked at them. "Why should you worry? You should have known that I would be here in my Father's house."

Jesus would have liked to stay, but he went back to Nazareth with his parents. He continued to grow both in stature and in wisdom and understanding. In all that he did, he pleased God and pleased those around him.

creative Fun

1. Make a copy of the finger puppets for each child in the group.
2. Color the puppets and cut them out.
3. Fold the puppets on the dotted lines.
4. Tape the edges together, leaving the bottom edge open.
5. Slip the puppets onto your fingers.
6. Retell the story of Jesus in the Temple.

Permission to photocopy for local church use. © 2005 Abingdon Press.

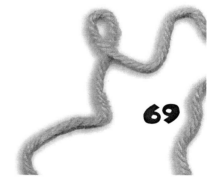

JESUS AND JOHN

The Bible
Luke 3:7-22

"You are my Son, the Beloved; with you I am well pleased."
(Luke 3:22)

Supplies
glue
paper
posterboard
scissors
pencils
colored art
tissue
tape
paper punch
yarn or string

Bible Story

John stood in the middle of the Jordan River. He called out to the people who stood around. "The kingdom of God is at hand. Ask for God's forgiveness, and be baptized."

Now John, Jesus' cousin, was a strange-looking man. But he wasn't concerned about his looks. He had a special job to do. God had sent him to prepare the way for God's only Son—the promised Messiah—and he took his job very seriously.

"You must change the way you are living. God does not want it to be this way. You have become thoughtless. You do not care whether other people have enough food to eat or clothes to wear. God's Promised One is coming. You will not be ready. Change your lives. Let the water wash you clean of all your wrong doings. Start again," he preached.

The people were worried. They did not want God's kingdom to come and them to be left out. They called out to him, "What shall we do to get ready?"

"Whoever has two coats, let him share with anyone who has none. Whoever has food should do the same. Tax collectors should stop cheating the people. Collect no more than what is due. Soldiers, be satisfied with your wages. Don't bully people into paying you extra," John told them.

Sometimes the people asked John if he were the Messiah, the one that God had promised.

"No," said John. "I am not the Messiah, but I have come to prepare his way. I'm not good enough even to bend down and untie his sandals."

One day, while John was preaching and baptizing, Jesus came to the bank of the Jordan River. John knew then that Jesus was the one that everyone had been waiting for.

"It is you who should baptize me," said John.

"Do it this way for now," Jesus told him. And John led Jesus into the water. When John poured the water over Jesus, the Spirit of God came upon Jesus like a dove, and a voice from heaven said, "You are my Son, the Beloved; with you I am well pleased."

creative fun

1. Cut out 2 hoops and 2 doves using the templates below.

2. Glue hoop onto tissue paper

colored tissue

3. Turn paper over and glue 2nd hoop into position

4. Trim tissue paper

5. glue dove into position

6. repeat on reverse (matching the doves exactly.)

7. Make a hole in the hoop and hang by a window.

Permission to photocopy for local church use. © 2004 Abingdon Press.

THE FISHERMEN

The Bible

Matthew 4:18-22

"Follow me, and I will make you fish for people."

(Matthew 4:19)

Supplies

glue
paper
scissors
crayons
markers
cardboard
    tubes
tissue paper
rubber bands

Bible Story

Refrain: **There are plenty of fish in the water.**
There are plenty of fish in the sea.
So I'm gonna throw out my net now,
And those fish will come swimmin' to me.

Simon and Andrew were brothers.
They went out in their boat every day.
They caught fish for the folks in the village.
If you listen you might hear them say: **(Refrain)**
Some days they caught fish by the hundreds.
Their baskets were filled to the rim.
The nets would be filled with each casting,
All day long till the sun's light grew dim. **(Refrain)**

But some days the nets came back empty.
There were hardly enough for a snack.
Though they fished and they fished and they fished,
Empty-handed the boats would come back. **(Refrain)**
But one day as the brothers were workin',
Putting all their equipment away,
Jesus came to the edge of the lakeshore,
"Follow me," is all that he'd say. **(Refrain)**

"If you'll come and be my disciples,
I'll teach you a new fishing skill.
Instead of those fish you'll catch people,
And I promise, catch people you will." **(Refrain)**
Peter stowed the hooks and the torches.
Andrew then put the old nets away.
The brothers left all they were doing
Just because of what Jesus did say. **(Refrain)**

"I have come to the lake to find helpers,
Who will carry my message to all.
James and John, I invite you to follow,
Join our group, be with us, one and all." **(Refrain)**
For Jesus had come to catch people,
To catch them and teach them God's ways.
To show them a new way of living—
God's kingdom would bring a new day. **(Refrain)**

creative Fun

1. Make a copy of the tube cover for each child.
2. Color the illustration. Cut it out.
3. Paint white glue onto a small cardboard tube.
4. Wrap the cover around the tube.
5. Cut a five-inch circle from tissue paper. Place the tissue over one end of the tube. Secure with a rubber band. Have the children hum into the tube.

Permission to photocopy for local church use. © 2005 Abingdon Press.

CALLING LEVI

the Bible

Mark 2:13-17

And Jesus said to him, "Follow me." (Mark 2:14, adapted)

supplies

two jars
pennies
paper
old crayons
variety of
  coins
masking tape
scissors

Bible Story

(Set out two jars, one labeled "ROME" and the other labeled "LEVI." Give each "taxpayer" three pennies to present.)

Taxpayer: We have added a new baby to our family. I've come to pay the tax.

Levi: That's two for Rome and one for Levi.

Taxpayer: I must take a trip to a nearby town to visit family. I've come to pay my road tax.

Levi: That's two for Rome and one for Levi.

Taxpayer: I have a vineyard on the outside of town. I am here to pay my vineyard tax.

Levi: That's two for Rome and one for Levi.

Taxpayer: I have just harvested my barley for the season. I have come to pay my harvest tax.

Levi: That's two for Rome and one for Levi.

Taxpayer: I have come to Jerusalem to go to the Temple to worship God. I've come to pay my Temple tax.

Levi: That's two for Rome and one for Levi.

Taxpayer: My family needs food. I've come to the market to shop. I've come to pay my market tax.

Levi: That's two for Rome and one for Levi.

Taxpayer: I have a small business selling copper pots. I've come to pay my business tax.

Levi: That's none for Rome and three for Levi.

Taxpayer: My daughter is getting married soon. She is marrying the carpenter of the village. I've come to pay my marriage tax.

Levi: That's none for Rome and three for Levi.

Jesus came to the market place that day. He knew what Levi was doing. Jesus said to him, "Levi, leave what you are doing and follow me. I need you."

And do you know what? Levi did. And Levi was so excited that he invited Jesus to come to dinner to meet his friends. Many of his friends were tax collectors too. The Pharisees who were in the marketplace grumbled about Jesus' choice of friends, but Jesus said, "People who are not sick don't need a doctor. I've come to help those who need my help."

And Jesus said to him, "Follow me."

(Mark 2:14, adapted)

CREATIVE FUN

1. Make a copy of the Bible verse poster for each child in the group.
2. Cut out the poster.
3. Put a loop of masking tape on the back of eight to ten coins (pennies, nickels, dimes, quarters, or even foreign currency).
4. Arrange the coins on the table.
5. Place the Bible verse poster over the coins.
6. Lightly tape the top so that it doesn't shift.
7. Remove the paper from old crayons.
8. Lay the crayons on their sides and rub over the Bible verse.

Permission to photocopy for local church use. © 2005 Abingdon Press.

JESUS PRAYS

the Bible

Luke 11:1-4

Lord, teach us to pray.
(Luke 11:1)

supplies

paper
crayons
markers
scissors
white glue
construction
paper or
drawing
paper

Bible story

Every day Jesus would go to a quiet place so that he could be alone with God. His disciples had seen him do this and wondered what he did. One day they asked him, "Where do you go when you leave the group?"

"There are so many people around all day long that I cannot be alone to talk to God. That is what I am doing," Jesus told them.

"But I thought by law we were to pray to God at certain times of the day and in certain places and using certain words," said one of the disciples.

"You can talk to God at any time and in any place," said Jesus. "God is always there. God will always be listening to you."

"What about the words?" asked another disciple. "Are there special words we should use like the prayers at the Temple?"

"Yes, and when you talk to God, do you look up to heaven, or do you bow your head? Please Jesus, teach us to pray."

"The prayers you pray in the Temple are loud and showy," said Jesus. "When you talk to God, you should do it quietly. Do not try to impress other people. Do not try to look smart or important. God already knows who you are. God knows what is in your heart. That is what is important."

"But are there special words we should say like the Temple prayers?" asked John.

"Prayer is something for God alone to hear. You do not need to use a lot of words when you pray. Just say what you need to say," answered Jesus.

"Can you tell us a prayer to use?" asked Nathaniel.

And Jesus told them this: *(Read the prayer on the following page.)*

"You must remember," Jesus added, "for God to forgive you for all the bad things you have done, you must forgive others who have done bad things to you." Jesus' friends were glad that they could talk to God anywhere and anytime.

Our Father,
who art in heaven,
hallowed be thy name.
Thy kingdom come,
thy will be done on earth
as it is in heaven.
Give us this day
our daily bread.
and forgive us our trespasses,
as we forgive those
who trespass against us.
And lead us not into temptation,
but deliver us from evil.
For thine is the kingdom,
and the power, and the glory,
forever.
Amen.

creative fun

1. Make a copy of the Lord's Prayer for each child.
2. Cut out the prayer and glue it into the center of a piece of drawing paper or construction paper.
3. Decorate the prayer.

Permission to photocopy for local church use. The Lord's Prayer is from *The United Methodist Hymnal*, © 1989 The United Methodist Publishing House.

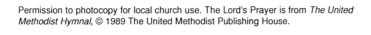

JAIRUS'S DAUGHTER

The Bible

Mark 5:21-43

In God I trust; I am not afraid.
(Psalm 56:11)

Supplies

paper
scissors
crayons
markers
construction
    paper
tape
pencil

Bible Story

One day a man named Jairus, who was a religious leader in the community, came to find Jesus. He had a wonderful family, but his daughter had become very, very sick. He and his wife did not think she would live much longer. Jairus had heard that Jesus was a healer. Perhaps Jesus could make his little girl well again.

Jairus ran as fast as he could to where Jesus was teaching. He threw himself down on the ground. "Please, oh, please, Jesus," Jairus begged. "Heal my little girl. She is dying. I need your help. I know if you place your hands on her she will be well again."

Jesus stood up and put his hand on Jairus's shoulder. Jairus knew that Jesus was going to help him. The two started back to Jairus's house. A whole crowd began to follow. They wanted to see what Jesus would do.

As they drew near the house a servant ran out to meet them. "It is too late! Your daughter has died. You don't have to bother the teacher anymore."

Jairus fell down to the ground in tears. His daughter, the love of his life, was gone. But Jesus didn't seem to pay any attention. "Don't be afraid," Jesus said to Jairus. "You must only believe. The little girl is not dead. She is just sleeping."

Jesus pushed through the crowd of mourners who had gathered at the house. He went into the room where the little girl was lying. He knelt down next to her pallet and took her hand. "Little girl, get up!"

The little girl sat up as though nothing had been wrong with her. Everyone stared in amazement. "Now get her something to eat," Jesus told them. Jairus could barely contain his joy. He wanted to tell everyone what Jesus had done.

Creative Fun

1. Make a copy of the two animal get-well figures for each child.
2. Color them with crayons or markers.

Line up center of animal to center of card, Tape down outside segment of animal!

3. Cut them out.
4. Fold each one down the center along the dotted lines.
5. Fold the legs forward on the dotted lines.
6. Cut construction paper sheets in half.
7. Fold each sheet in the middle, making a 4" by 6" card.
8. Sandwich the animal in the card, matching the center fold of the card and the center fold of the animal. (See diagram above.)
9. Tape the legs of either animal to the inside of the card.
10. Write a get-well message inside.

We may not be able to heal someone, but we can send people get-well messages.

Permission to photocopy for local church use. © 1997 Abingdon Press.

THE BOY'S LUNCH

the Bible

John 6:1-14

Do not neglect to do good
and to share what you have.
(Hebrews 13:16)

supplies
paper
scissors
crayons
markers
paper punch
yarn
masking tape

Bible story

Everywhere Jesus went the people would follow. They followed him down the road. They followed him to the cities. They followed him through the countryside. Jesus could never get away from people.

One day when Jesus was particularly tired, he and his friends got into a boat to cross the lake and get away, but the people followed the boat around to the other side of the lake. When Jesus and his friends put the boat onto the beach, there were the people waiting for him.

Jesus felt sorry for them and did not send them away. He gathered them together and began to teach them. All day long more and more people came to see him. Soon there were more than five thousand people.

When Jesus finished teaching the people, it was late in the day. Jesus was tired. Jesus' friends were tired. The people were tired. And everyone was hungry.

"What are we going to do about food?" asked one of the disciples. "It's getting late and there is nothing here for the people to eat. Shall I send them into the nearby village for food?"

"No, we should provide for them," said Jesus. "They are tired and hungry. They have already come a long way."

"We don't have enough money to buy bread, even a small amount, for such a large group of people. What shall we do?" asked the disciples.

Just then a small boy stepped forward. He held out his leather lunch pouch. "Here. I will share my lunch."

The boy had been in the crowd. He had come a long way as well. He had brought with him only five small barley loaves and two dried fish. This was hardly enough to feed a hungry boy, much less over five thousand people. But Jesus took the lunch. He gave thanks to God and broke the bread. Then he passed the lunch around to the people.

When the people had eaten all they cared to eat, Jesus had his friends gather up the leftover food. What a wonderful thing had happened! There were twelve full baskets left over. It was a miracle!

80

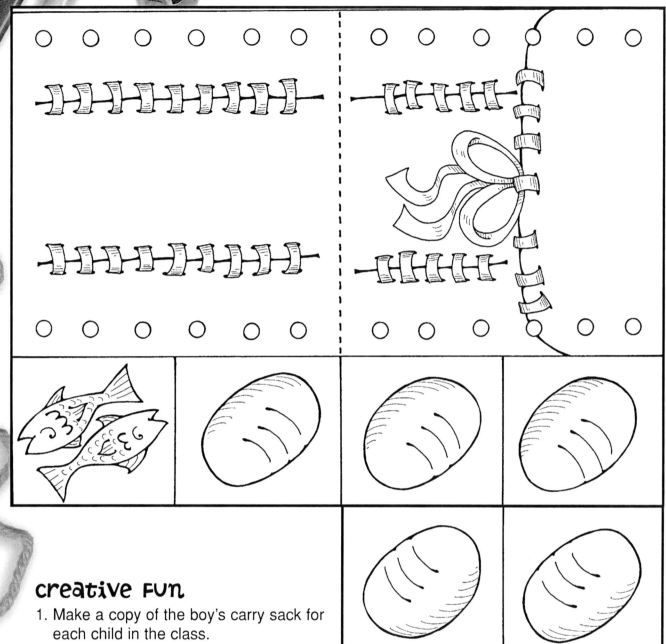

creative FUN

1. Make a copy of the boy's carry sack for each child in the class.
2. Cut out the carry sack and fold on the dotted lines. Color the sack.
3. Using a paper punch, punch holes where shown.
4. Cut a piece of yarn thirty-six inches long. Wrap one end with a piece of masking tape. Tape the other end to the inside of the carry sack.
5. Sew one side of the carry sack together. At the top of the first side, leave a twenty-inch strip of yarn for the handle.
6. Continue down the second side of the sack. Tape the end of the yarn to the inside.
7. Cut out the bread and fish. Color them and then place them inside the carry sack.

Remember how the boy shared his lunch.

Permission to photocopy for local church use. © 1997 Abingdon Press.

THE LOST SHEEP

The Bible
Matthew 18:12-14

We are his people, and the sheep of his pasture.
(Psalm 100:3)

Supplies
paper
scissors
crayons
markers
tape
plastic drinking
    straws
stapler, staples

Bible Story
Response: Baa, baa, baa.

Once there was a shepherd who had one hundred sheep.
He led them to cool water and green grass for them to eat.
(Response)
"Come, my sheep," the shepherd said, "Let's go out for the day.
The sun is warm and the grass is fresh. You can run and play.
And when the sun begins to set, and the sky's no longer light,
We'll come back down the mountain to the fold to spend the night."
(Response)
One, two, three, four, five and six, seven, eight, and nine.
The shepherd counted every one, 'till he got to ninety-nine.
"I must have counted wrong," he said, and counted them again.
But all he found were ninety-nine, standing in the pen.
(Response)
"Today there were one hundred sheep!" he cried in great distress.
"If one is missing from the flock, I'll be in such a mess."
The shepherd left the ninety-nine to search for that one sheep.
He had to find the missing one before he went to sleep.
(Response)
"He could have fallen off the cliff or been eaten by a bear;
He could have fallen in the stream and drowned with me not there."
"There you are," the shepherd said, when the little one he spied.
"Don't move a muscle or you'll fall," the frightened shepherd cried.
(Response)
He scooped the missing sheep right up into his waiting arms.
"I'll take you home," the shepherd said, "back where it's safe and warm.
"Let's celebrate," the shepherd said, "I've found my long lost sheep.
And now that we are home again, I know that I can sleep."
(Response)
When Jesus told this story, to people long ago,
He wanted them to know that their Shepherd loves them so.
(Response)

Creative Fun

1. Make a copy of the shepherd and sheep for each child.
2. Cut out the card and fold along the dotted line.
3. Color the shepherd and the sheep.
4. Open the card and tape a plastic drinking straw to the inside back of one of the pictures. One end of the straw should extend about four inches below the edge of the card.
5. Close the card. Tape or staple the edges together. Make sure to get close to the place where the straw extends.
6. Hold the straw between the palms of your hands. Roll it back and forth and help the shepherd find his lost sheep.

Permission to photocopy for local church use. © 1998 Abingdon Press.

THE GOOD NEIGHBOR

The Bible

Luke 10:25-37

You shall love your neighbor as yourself.
(Matthew 22:39)

Supplies

paper
scissors
crayons
markers
tape
construction paper
plastic drinking straws

Bible Story

A man was going down to Jericho. As he traveled, he was attacked by robbers who beat him, took his clothes, and left him for dead beside the road. As it happened, a priest was going down the road. The injured man thought to himself, "He is a priest. Surely he will help me."

When the priest saw the man lying there, he went to the far side of the road. "If I pretend that I don't see him, then I won't have to help him. I don't have time today. I'm in a hurry," said the priest. And he walked quickly past, looking the other way.

A little while later a Levite came down the road. The injured man thought to himself, "Here comes a Levite. He will take pity on me and help me."

But the Levite saw the injured man and looked away. He didn't have time today to help him. Besides, it would be too much trouble. He walked quickly past, looking the other way.

Some time later a Samaritan traveled down the road. The injured man looked up and thought to himself, "This Samaritan won't help me. Why should I even hope?"

The Samaritan saw the injured man. He stopped to help. He bandaged the man's wounds, and then set him on his own donkey. They traveled to a nearby inn. There the Samaritan told the innkeeper to take care of him. "I will repay you whatever more you spend."

Which of these three was the good neighbor?

Creative Fun

1. Make a copy of the story background and figures for each child.
2. Cut out the top picture. Color it.
3. Glue or tape it to a piece of construction paper.
4. Cut out the strip with the injured traveler. Color it.
5. Glue or tape the ends to the same piece of construction paper, overlapping the story background slightly. Leave the center free.
6. Color and cut out each of the figures.

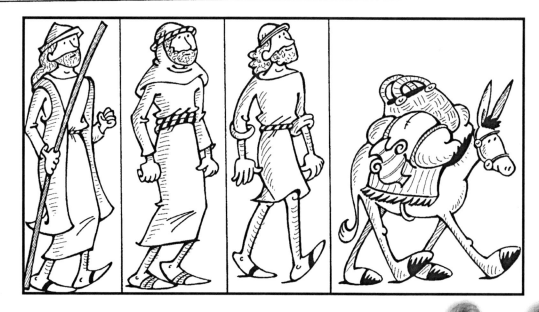

7. Mount each figure to a plastic drinking straw.
8. Slip the figures between the background and the traveler's strip to tell the story of the Good Samaritan.

Permission to photocopy for local church use. © 1998 Abingdon Press.

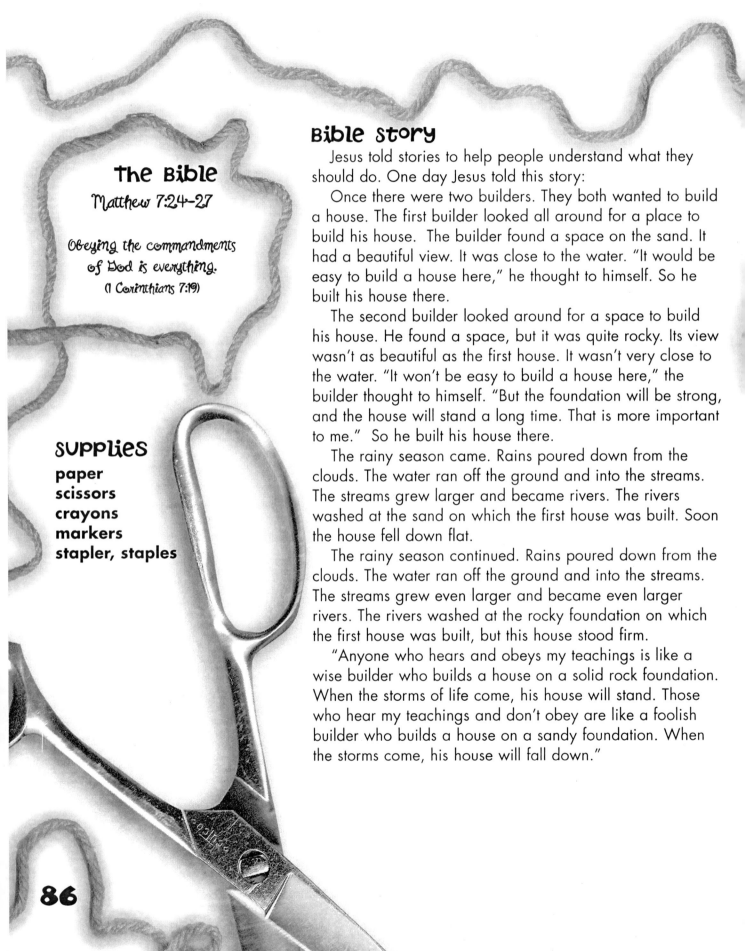

TWO HOUSES

The Bible

Matthew 7:24-27

Obeying the commandments of God is everything.
(1 Corinthians 7:19)

Supplies

paper
scissors
crayons
markers
stapler, staples

Bible Story

Jesus told stories to help people understand what they should do. One day Jesus told this story:

Once there were two builders. They both wanted to build a house. The first builder looked all around for a place to build his house. The builder found a space on the sand. It had a beautiful view. It was close to the water. "It would be easy to build a house here," he thought to himself. So he built his house there.

The second builder looked around for a space to build his house. He found a space, but it was quite rocky. Its view wasn't as beautiful as the first house. It wasn't very close to the water. "It won't be easy to build a house here," the builder thought to himself. "But the foundation will be strong, and the house will stand a long time. That is more important to me." So he built his house there.

The rainy season came. Rains poured down from the clouds. The water ran off the ground and into the streams. The streams grew larger and became rivers. The rivers washed at the sand on which the first house was built. Soon the house fell down flat.

The rainy season continued. Rains poured down from the clouds. The water ran off the ground and into the streams. The streams grew even larger and became even larger rivers. The rivers washed at the rocky foundation on which the first house was built, but this house stood firm.

"Anyone who hears and obeys my teachings is like a wise builder who builds a house on a solid rock foundation. When the storms of life come, his house will stand. Those who hear my teachings and don't obey are like a foolish builder who builds a house on a sandy foundation. When the storms come, his house will fall down."

CREATIVE FUN

1. Make a copy of the flip book cards for each child in the class.
2. Color the pictures of the two houses.
3. Cut the cards apart.
4. Stack them with card number one on the bottom. Card number twelve should be on the top.
5. Staple the cards together.
6. Flip the pages and watch what happens.

Permission to photocopy for local church use. © 1998 Abingdon Press.

A LOVING FATHER

the Bible
Luke 15:11-32

God's steadfast love endures forever.
(Psalm 107:1, adapted)

supplies
paper
scissors
crayons
markers

Bible story
Jesus told the following story to help the people know what God was like.

Once there was a father who had two sons. The older son was hard-working and obedient. The younger son was impatient and reckless.

One day the younger son came to his father, "I know that some day part of your land will be mine. I am young. I've got a lot of living to do. I don't want to wait."

Now the father loved both of his sons very much. He knew that his youngest son was making a poor choice. But he wanted to make his son happy, so he gave the younger son his share of the inheritance.

The younger son went off to the city. There he spent his money unwisely on clothing and good times. He had many friends who helped him spend his money, but one day the money ran out and so did the friends.

The younger son was starving, so he went to work for a farmer who raised pigs. The younger son even ate the left-over food that was given to the pigs. He was so unhappy. He had no money, no friends, no home, no food.

"Even my father's servants live better than this. I'm going back home. If I cannot be his son again, then I will be his servant." So the younger son said goodbye to the pigs and the pig farmer and started for home.

When the boy came near his father's house, he received a big surprise. His father came running out to greet him. His father welcomed him home and gave him new sandals and a new robe. He had a party to welcome the boy home.

The people who heard this story learned that like the father in the story, God forgave them and welcomed them back whenever they did wrong.

creative fun
1. Make a copy of the storybook for each child.
2. Cut out the storybook and fold on the dotted lines.
3. Draw pictures of each part of the story.

The younger son took his inheritance and went into the city. In a very short time he had spent all the money.

The younger son found himself without friends, without food, and without a place to stay. "I'm going home," said the son. "Even my father's servants live better than this."

God's steadfast love endures forever.
(Psalm 107:1, adapted)

The Forgiving Father

His father welcomed him home with open arms. From this story Jesus wanted the people to know that God was loving and forgiving.

Once there was a father who had two sons. The younger son was impatient and restless. One day he went to his father and demanded that he be given his inheritance.

Permission to photocopy for local church use. © 2005 Abingdon Press.

GREAT COMMANDMENT

The Bible

Matthew 22:34-40

Love the Lord your God with all your heart, and with all your soul, and with all your mind.

(Matthew 22:37)

Supplies

paper
crayons
markers
tape or glue

Bible Story

The things that Jesus taught were often different from what the people were used to. Some people liked what Jesus had to say. Others wondered by whose authority he spoke. Others thought him to be a troublemaker and wanted to get rid of him. Many times religious leaders would try to trick Jesus into saying something wrong. Then they could have him arrested.

One day while Jesus was teaching, a group of Pharisees decided to ask him a question. "Teacher, which commandment is the greatest in the law?"

The Pharisees smiled to themselves. If Jesus chose any one of the commandments to be greater than any other one, then he would be in trouble. He would be teaching against the Law of Moses, where all the commandments are equally important.

Jesus thought for a moment. Everyone around him was waiting expectantly to see what he would say. "You shall love the Lord your God with all your heart, and with all your soul, and with all your mind. This is the first and greatest commandment. And a second is very much like it: You shall love your neighbor as yourself."

The Pharisees were stumped. The commandment that Jesus had listed as the greatest commandment and the second commandment actually summarized all the commandments that were included in the Law of Moses.

Creative Fun

1. Make a copy of this envelope for each child.
2. Color the envelope.
3. Cut it out and fold the tabs down on the dotted line.
4. Tape or glue the sides of the envelope together.
5. Take the envelope home and find ways to earn money to help others. When the envelope is full, bring it back to church. Give it to the church mission projects.

You shall love your neighbor as yourself.

Matthew 22:39

I treasure your word in my heart.

Psalm 119:11

You shall love the Lord your God with all your heart.

Luke 10:27

Permission to photocopy for local church use. © 1998 Abingdon Press.

JESUS AND THE CHILDREN

the Bible

Mark 10:13–16

Let the little children come to me.
(Mark 10:14)

Supplies

paper
scissors
markers
crayons
pencils

Bible Story

"Have you heard? Have you heard? Jesus is coming!" The news spread to all the women at the well.

"Jesus is coming? We must go to see him! We will take the children. Maybe Jesus will bless them." The women hurried to their homes and gathered up their children. They went to the place where Jesus was teaching.

Already a big crowd was there. The mothers and their children tried to get closer to Jesus. "Please let us through," they said. "We would like for Jesus to bless our children."

Some of Jesus' friends stood on the outside of the crowd. They saw the women and children. "Go away," they said. "Jesus has been teaching all day. He is tired. He doesn't have time for children!"

Sadly the women and the children turned away. They had come a long way to see Jesus. They were so disappointed.

But then the women and children heard a voice. "Don't send these children away. Let them come here!" Jesus scolded the men who had sent the women and children away.

The crowd made way for the mothers and their children to come forward. They ran to Jesus. He took them on his lap. Jesus touched their heads and blessed them. They knew that Jesus loved them.

"It is to children such as these that the kingdom of God belongs. Whoever doesn't receive the kingdom as a child will never enter it."

creative fun

1. Make a copy of the "welcome" card for each child.
2. Cut out the card and color it.
3. Fold on the dotted lines.
4. Write a welcome message for someone who might be visiting your church or Sunday school class.

Jesus welcomed the children who were not usually included. How can you make people feel welcome at church?

Permission to photocopy for local church use. © 2005 Abingdon Press.

ZACCHAEUS

The Bible
Luke 19:1–10

For the Son of Man came to seek out and to save the lost.
(Luke 19:10)

Supplies
paper
scissors
crayons
markers
tape
drawing paper

Bible Story

Zacchaeus was a tax collector, which means that nobody liked him very much. Most tax collectors were dishonest, and Zacchaeus was no exception to the rule. He would collect the taxes for the Romans, and then he would slip a few coins for himself in his own pocket.

One day Zacchaeus was at his tax table when he heard the news. Jesus, the Teacher, was coming to town. Now, Zacchaeus had heard about Jesus. He had heard about the things Jesus said. He had heard about the things Jesus did. Zacchaeus wanted to see this man for himself.

So, Zacchaeus closed up his tax table and went to the road to catch a glimpse of Jesus as he passed by. But Zacchaeus wasn't the only one who had come to see Jesus. Hundreds of others lined the road as well.

Zacchaeus was a short, little man and standing at the back of the crowd was not appealing to him. He would not be able to see. He tried to push his way to the front, but the people wouldn't let him through.

Then Zacchaeus saw a rather large sycamore tree. Its limbs hung out over the road. Surely if he climbed up there, he would be able to see just fine. So, up, up, up Zacchaeus went. He scooted out onto one of the strong limbs and sat there until Jesus came by.

Instead of passing the tree and going on his way, Jesus stopped right beneath the limb where Zacchaeus was sitting. "Zacchaeus, come down here right now!" Jesus said to him. "I'm coming to your house for dinner tonight."

Zacchaeus could hardly believe Jesus was speaking to him. But he hurried down the tree and hurried home to get everything ready. Zacchaeus knew that some changes in his life were in order. That night Zacchaeus promised to change his life. He would give half of his possessions to the poor. "And if I have cheated anyone, I will pay them back four times as much," he promised.

Jesus smiled, " I came to this world to look for people who are lost. I'm glad I found you today, Zacchaeus."

creative fun

1. Make a copy of the tree for each child in the class.
2. Color the tree and then cut it out.
3. With assistance, cut the door in the center of the tree.
4. Cut drawing paper slightly larger than the size of the opening in the tree.
5. Draw something you might find in a tree.
6. Tape the drawing to the back of the open space.
7. Play a guessing game, giving clues as to what might be in the tree. Open the door to discover the answer.

Permission to photocopy for local church use. © 1998 Abingdon Press.

THE FOUR FRIENDS

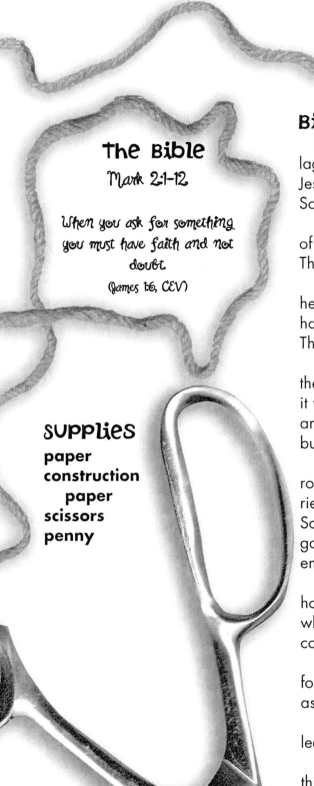

The Bible
Mark 2:1-12

When you ask for something you must have faith and not doubt.

(James 1:6, CEV)

Supplies
**paper
construction
   paper
scissors
penny**

Bible Story

One day word spread that Jesus was coming to the village of Capernaum. Because of all the wonderful things Jesus had done, he was all that anyone ever talked about. So when the word got out, everyone came to see him.

Jesus was staying in a house in Capernaum. But because of all the people, the little house became very crowded. There was hardly any room to breathe, much less move.

Some men in the village had heard about Jesus. They had heard how he healed the sick and raised the dead. They had a friend who had been paralyzed since he was born. They wanted Jesus to make their friend well.

The men put their friend on a pallet and carried him to the house where Jesus was staying. But when they got there, it was so crowded that they could not get in. They shouted, and still Jesus did not hear them. They pushed and pushed, but no one would let them through the crowd.

Just then one of the men got an idea. "Let's go up to the roof. I know how we can get our friend inside." They carried their friend up the outside stairway to the flat roof. Scrape, scrape, scrape. No one below could hear what was going on on the roof. Soon there was a hole, a hole big enough for their friend and his bed.

The four men slowly lowered their friend's bed through the hole in the roof. They lowered him to a spot right in front of where Jesus was standing. Jesus looked up at the men. He could see the great faith the men had in what he could do.

"Friend," Jesus said to the man on the mat, "Your sins are forgiven. Take up your bed and walk." Everyone was amazed as the man got up from his mat and walked away.

"Who is this? Only God can forgive sins!" some of the leaders of the synagogue said.

"I speak with the power of God to forgive sins and make this man well," Jesus told them. Everyone was happy except the Pharisees and scribes who believed that Jesus had said something terribly wrong.

creative fun

1. Make a copy of the picture of Jesus and the four friends for each child.
2. Cut a piece of construction paper the exact same size as the picture.
3. Cut the construction paper into ten to twelve pieces for roof "tiles."
4. Place the pieces over the picture, totally covering it.
5. Find a friend to play the game with you.
6. Toss a penny. If it comes up heads, you can remove two tiles from the roof. If it comes up tails, you can remove one tile from the roof. See who removes all the tiles from the roof first.

Permission to photocopy for local church use. © 1997 Abingdon Press.

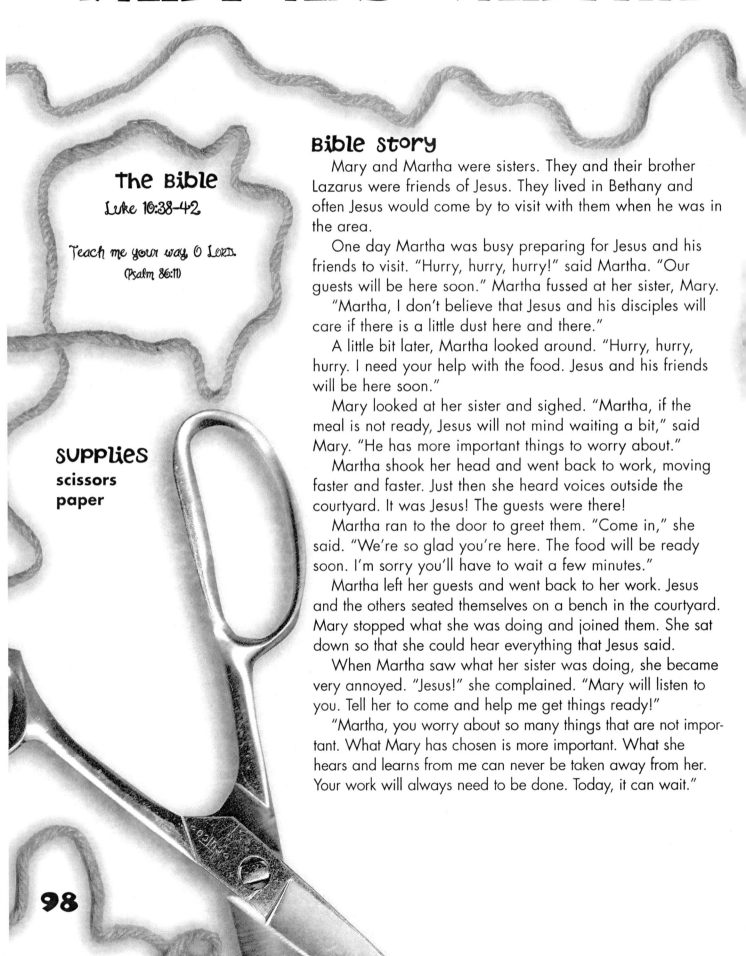

MARY AND MARTHA

The Bible

Luke 10:38-42

Teach me your way, O Lord.
(Psalm 86:11)

Supplies
scissors
paper

Bible Story

Mary and Martha were sisters. They and their brother Lazarus were friends of Jesus. They lived in Bethany and often Jesus would come by to visit with them when he was in the area.

One day Martha was busy preparing for Jesus and his friends to visit. "Hurry, hurry, hurry!" said Martha. "Our guests will be here soon." Martha fussed at her sister, Mary.

"Martha, I don't believe that Jesus and his disciples will care if there is a little dust here and there."

A little bit later, Martha looked around. "Hurry, hurry, hurry. I need your help with the food. Jesus and his friends will be here soon."

Mary looked at her sister and sighed. "Martha, if the meal is not ready, Jesus will not mind waiting a bit," said Mary. "He has more important things to worry about."

Martha shook her head and went back to work, moving faster and faster. Just then she heard voices outside the courtyard. It was Jesus! The guests were there!

Martha ran to the door to greet them. "Come in," she said. "We're so glad you're here. The food will be ready soon. I'm sorry you'll have to wait a few minutes."

Martha left her guests and went back to her work. Jesus and the others seated themselves on a bench in the courtyard. Mary stopped what she was doing and joined them. She sat down so that she could hear everything that Jesus said.

When Martha saw what her sister was doing, she became very annoyed. "Jesus!" she complained. "Mary will listen to you. Tell her to come and help me get things ready!"

"Martha, you worry about so many things that are not important. What Mary has chosen is more important. What she hears and learns from me can never be taken away from her. Your work will always need to be done. Today, it can wait."

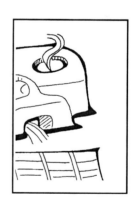

creative fun

1. Make a copy of this page for each child in the class.
2. Cut the items apart. Find the two halves that go together.

Each of these items would have been used by Martha or Mary in preparing a meal. Can you find the broom? the clay cooking stove? the water jar? the lamp? the clay oven? the grain hand mill? the palm basket? the reed mat?

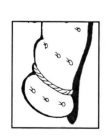

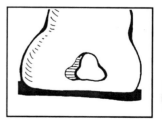

Permission to photocopy for local church use. © 2000 Abingdon Press.

HOSANNA!

The Bible

Mark 11:1-11

Hosanna! Blessed is the one who comes in the name of the Lord.

(Mark 11:9)

Supplies

paper
scissors
white glue
plastic straws
crayons

Bible Story

"Philip! Andrew! I've got a job for you!" Jesus called to his friends. "Go into the village up the road. There you will find a small donkey. Untie it and bring it to me."

"What if someone thinks we're stealing it?" asked Philip. He didn't want to get into any trouble, not now anyway.

"Just tell them that the Lord needs it," Jesus answered.

Philip and Andrew set off for the village. When they found the donkey, Philip began to untie it.

"Why are you untying that donkey?" the owner asked. "What are you going to do with it?"

"The Lord needs it," said Andrew. And the owner let him lead the donkey away.

Andrew and Philip led the donkey back to where Jesus was. They threw their cloaks on its back and Jesus climbed on. They started down the road. Jesus' friends followed close behind.

When Jesus and his friends got closer to the city, the people along the way began to whisper to one another and point. "Look! Isn't that Jesus? Is Jesus coming to Jerusalem?"

"Who is Jesus?" asked some.

"Jesus the healer. Jesus the teacher. Jesus the prophet from Nazareth. Jesus the Son of God, the Messiah. He is coming to Jerusalem for the Passover!" others answered.

News of Jesus spread among the people. Soon people were waiting and watching for him. They cut palm branches from the trees and waved them in the air. They laid their cloaks on the ground for the donkey to walk on.

"Hosanna! Hosanna!" the people shouted. "Blessed is the one who comes in the name of the Lord!"

Creative Fun

1. Make two copies of the palm leaf for each child.
2. Color both palm leaves and then cut them out.
3. Tape a plastic drinking straw down the inside center of one of the the palm leaves. Leave about two inches of the straw extending beyond the end of the palm branch.

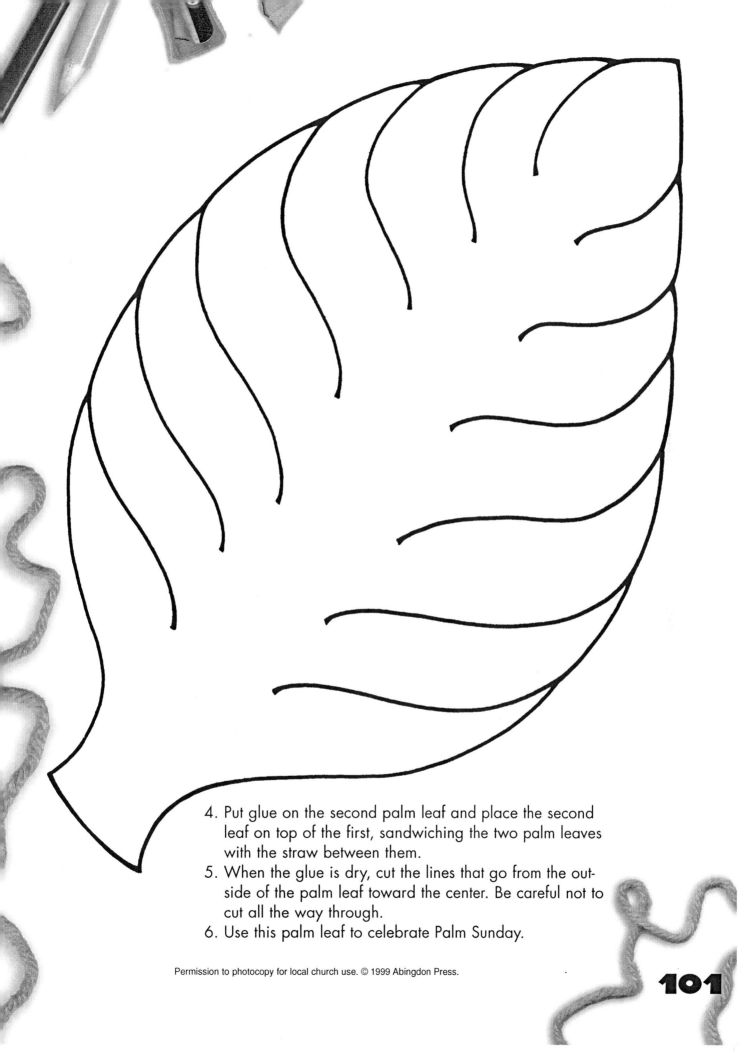

4. Put glue on the second palm leaf and place the second leaf on top of the first, sandwiching the two palm leaves with the straw between them.
5. When the glue is dry, cut the lines that go from the outside of the palm leaf toward the center. Be careful not to cut all the way through.
6. Use this palm leaf to celebrate Palm Sunday.

Permission to photocopy for local church use. © 1999 Abingdon Press.

REMEMBER ME

The Bible

Matthew 26:17-29;
John 13:4-6

Do this in remembrance
of me.
(1 Corinthians 11:24)

Supplies

**paper
scissors
crayons
markers
cotton swabs
baby oil
small containers**

Bible Story

Getting ready for the Passover was not easy. Everything in the house had to be spotlessly clean. Special foods had to be prepared in special ways. Even though Jesus and his friends were from out of town, still they had to follow the special rules.

Peter and John asked Jesus, "Where are we going to make the preparations to celebrate Passover?"

"Go into the city. There you will see a man carrying a water jar. Follow him. He will lead you to the house where we will eat the Passover meal."

Peter and John found the man. They followed him back to his house. Peter and John began to get ready.

The sun was going down. The disciples found their way to the upper room where the meal was being served. As they arrived, there was no servant to clean their feet. So Jesus got up from the table, took off his outer robe, tied a towel around himself, and picked up the basin. He began to wash the feet of his friends.

When Jesus came to Peter, Peter stopped him. "No, Lord, this is not right. You shouldn't be doing the work of a servant."

"Peter, unless you let me wash your feet, then you are no follower of mine," said Jesus.

"Then Lord, wash not only my feet but also my hands and my head," said Peter.

When Jesus finished, he put on his robe again. "Do you see what I have done? I have set an example for you to follow. You must learn to serve each other. Do as I have done."

That night after the Passover meal, Jesus took the bread. He broke it and gave some to each of his friends. "Eat this. This represents my body, which will soon be broken. Do this in remembrance of me."

Then he took the wine and poured it into a cup. He passed it to each of them. "Drink this. This represents my blood. Do this in remembrance of me. From now on, when you eat the bread and drink from the cup, remember me. Remember the example I have set for you." The disciples wondered what was about to happen.

creative fun

1. Make a copy of the stained glass window for each child.
2. Color the window with permanent markers or crayons.
3. Cut out the window.
4. Pour a small amount of baby oil into small containers.
5. Dip the cotton swab in the baby oil and rub it over the picture.
6. Place the stained glass window in a sunny location.

Permission to photocopy for local church use. © 2003 Abingdon Press.

A ROOSTER CROWS

the Bible
Mark 14:26-31, 66-72

I do not know this man.
(Mark 14:71)

supplies
paper
white glue
scissors
crayons
markers
wooden craft
   sticks
tape

Bible Story

**Refrain: *Cock-a-doodle-doodle. Cock-a-doodle-do!
Peter broke his promise. Now what will he do?***

*(Have the children create the rooster prior to the Bible story.
They can make the rooster crow on the refrain.)*
To the grove the soldiers rushed with swords and spears
   held high.
All the others ran away, but Peter stayed close by.
They led their prisoner down the street. His hands and feet
   were bound.
They brought him to the high priest's house; the council
   gathered 'round. **(Refrain)**

"You say you are the Son of God, the Son of God Most High!"
Jesus said, "That's what YOU say." "We've heard him,"
   people lied.
Peter stood outside the house, for he was Jesus' friend.
He wondered what would happen when the trial came to an
   end. **(Refrain)**

A serving girl saw Peter. The fire lit up his face.
"You look like someone I have seen, but in another place.
I think you are the prisoner's friend," and Peter turned away.
"I do not know of whom you speak. You're wrong in what
   you say." **(Refrain)**

"I believe the girl is right. Your voice gives you away.
You sound just like him," someone said, "Don't turn your
   face away."
"I do not know him," Peter cried, and moved away from them.
"You are wrong in what you say. I DO NOT KNOW HIM!"
   (Refrain)

The sky was getting lighter. The day would soon be here.
A rooster climbed upon the wall. He sang out loud and clear.
When Peter heard the rooster, he felt his heart would break.
Those words "I do not know him!" meant he'd broken the
   vow he'd made.

creative FUN

1. Make a copy of the
   rooster for each child.
2. Color the rooster in
   bright colors and then cut it out.
3. Fold the rooster in half.
4. Tape a wooden craft stick or a folded piece of construction paper inside
   the rooster to serve as a handle.
5. Staple or glue around the edges.
6. Use the rooster with the refrain of the Bible story.

Permission to photocopy for local church use. © 2003 Abingdon Press.

JESUS LIVES!

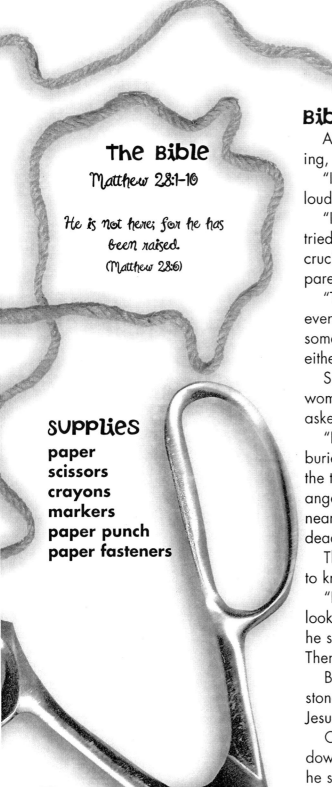

The Bible

Matthew 28:1–10

He is not here; for he has been raised.
(Matthew 28:6)

Supplies

paper
scissors
crayons
markers
paper punch
paper fasteners

Bible Story

After the sabbath, as the first day of the week was dawning, Mary Magdalene and the other Mary went to the tomb.

"I can't believe Jesus is dead," Mary Magdalene said out loud. "What will we do now?"

"It was all so quick. Arrested in the middle of the night, tried before the council, and even taken to Pilate. He was crucified and in the tomb before we even had time to prepare his body for burial," said the other Mary.

"The least we can do is show him the proper respect, even if the authorities didn't allow it. I hope there will be someone to roll back the stone. It is much too heavy for either one of us," said Mary Magdalene.

Suddenly the earth began to tremble and shake. The two women clung to each other in fear. "What was that?" they asked each other.

"Look," said Mary, pointing to the spot where Jesus was buried. The large round stone had been rolled aside. Beside the tomb sat an angel. The two women knew he must be an angel because he was as bright as lightning. On the ground nearby were the guards. They looked as though they were dead, but they were only unconscious.

The two women walked closer to the tomb. They wanted to know what had happened to their friend Jesus.

"Don't be afraid," said the angel. "I know that you're looking for Jesus. He isn't here. He has been raised, just as he said he would be. Come, see the place where he lay. Then go quickly and tell the others."

Both Marys peeked into the dark tomb. There on the stone bench were the cloths that had been wrapped around Jesus. Truly he was gone. He *had* been raised.

On the road back to the city, they ran into Jesus. They fell down to the ground and grabbed his feet. "Don't be afraid," he said. "Go and tell all my friends to go to Galilee. There they will find me." Then he left.

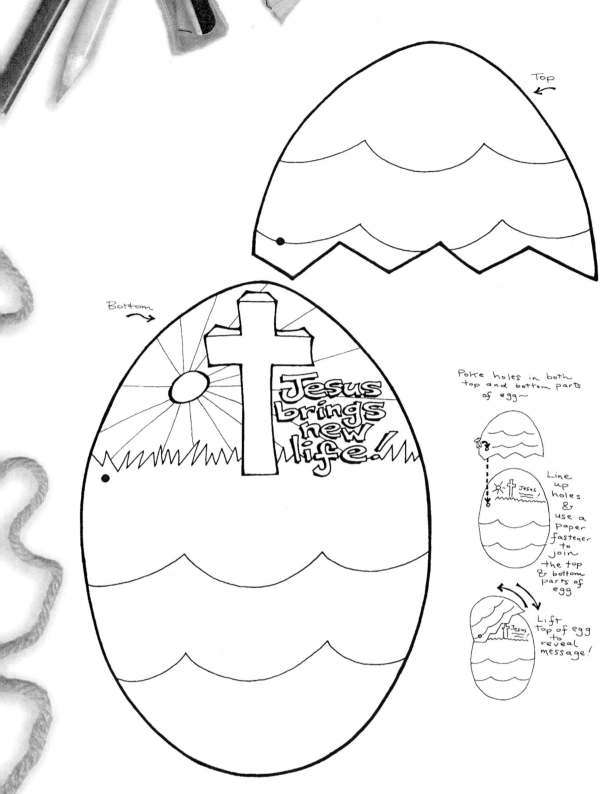

Top

Bottom

Jesus brings new life!

Poke holes in both top and bottom parts of egg~

Line up holes & use a Paper fastener to join the top & bottom parts of egg

Lift top of egg to reveal message!

creative FUN

1. Make a copy of the Easter egg for each child in the class.
2. Color the Easter egg and cut out the two parts.
3. Punch two holes where indicated on the egg base and the egg top.
4. Attach the top of the egg to the egg base using a paper fastener.
5. Lift the top of the egg to reveal the message.

The Easter egg became a symbol of the new life brought by Jesus' resurrection.

Permission to photocopy for local church use. © 1999 Abingdon Press.

THE EMMAUS ROAD

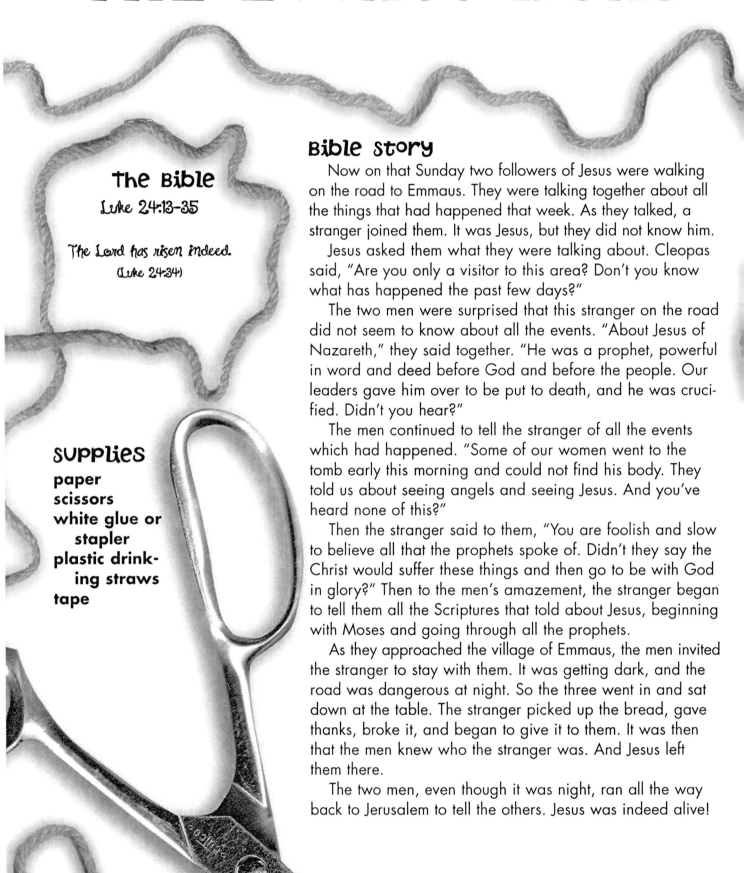

The Bible

Luke 24:13-35

The Lord has risen indeed.
(Luke 24:34)

Supplies

paper
scissors
white glue or
    stapler
plastic drink-
    ing straws
tape

Bible Story

Now on that Sunday two followers of Jesus were walking on the road to Emmaus. They were talking together about all the things that had happened that week. As they talked, a stranger joined them. It was Jesus, but they did not know him.

Jesus asked them what they were talking about. Cleopas said, "Are you only a visitor to this area? Don't you know what has happened the past few days?"

The two men were surprised that this stranger on the road did not seem to know about all the events. "About Jesus of Nazareth," they said together. "He was a prophet, powerful in word and deed before God and before the people. Our leaders gave him over to be put to death, and he was cruci-fied. Didn't you hear?"

The men continued to tell the stranger of all the events which had happened. "Some of our women went to the tomb early this morning and could not find his body. They told us about seeing angels and seeing Jesus. And you've heard none of this?"

Then the stranger said to them, "You are foolish and slow to believe all that the prophets spoke of. Didn't they say the Christ would suffer these things and then go to be with God in glory?" Then to the men's amazement, the stranger began to tell them all the Scriptures that told about Jesus, beginning with Moses and going through all the prophets.

As they approached the village of Emmaus, the men invited the stranger to stay with them. It was getting dark, and the road was dangerous at night. So the three went in and sat down at the table. The stranger picked up the bread, gave thanks, broke it, and began to give it to them. It was then that the men knew who the stranger was. And Jesus left them there.

The two men, even though it was night, ran all the way back to Jerusalem to tell the others. Jesus was indeed alive!

creative fun

1. Make a copy of the thaumatrope.
2. Cut out the thaumatrope and fold it on the dotted line.
3. Tape a plastic drinking straw securely to the inside of the thaumatrope. Make sure the straw extends about four inches beyond the bottom of the card.
4. Glue or staple the edges together.
5. Hold the straw between the palms of your hand.
6. Roll the straw back and forth and watch the figure of Jesus join the two men on the road to Emmaus.

Permission to photocopy for local church use. © 2003 Cokesbury.

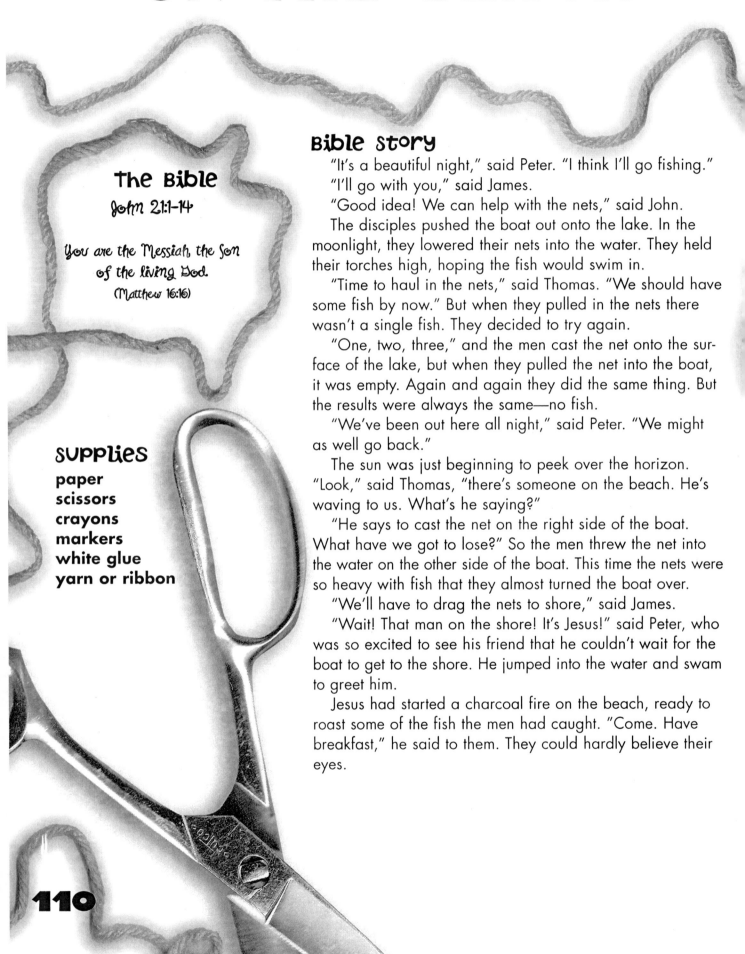

ON THE BEACH

The Bible

John 21:1-14

You are the Messiah, the Son of the living God.

(Matthew 16:16)

Supplies

paper
scissors
crayons
markers
white glue
yarn or ribbon

Bible Story

"It's a beautiful night," said Peter. "I think I'll go fishing."

"I'll go with you," said James.

"Good idea! We can help with the nets," said John.

The disciples pushed the boat out onto the lake. In the moonlight, they lowered their nets into the water. They held their torches high, hoping the fish would swim in.

"Time to haul in the nets," said Thomas. "We should have some fish by now." But when they pulled in the nets there wasn't a single fish. They decided to try again.

"One, two, three," and the men cast the net onto the surface of the lake, but when they pulled the net into the boat, it was empty. Again and again they did the same thing. But the results were always the same—no fish.

"We've been out here all night," said Peter. "We might as well go back."

The sun was just beginning to peek over the horizon. "Look," said Thomas, "there's someone on the beach. He's waving to us. What's he saying?"

"He says to cast the net on the right side of the boat. What have we got to lose?" So the men threw the net into the water on the other side of the boat. This time the nets were so heavy with fish that they almost turned the boat over.

"We'll have to drag the nets to shore," said James.

"Wait! That man on the shore! It's Jesus!" said Peter, who was so excited to see his friend that he couldn't wait for the boat to get to the shore. He jumped into the water and swam to greet him.

Jesus had started a charcoal fire on the beach, ready to roast some of the fish the men had caught. "Come. Have breakfast," he said to them. They could hardly believe their eyes.

I can share the good news about Jesus with others

creative FUN

1. Make two copies of the mobile parts for each child in the class.
2. Have the children color the pictures and then cut them out.
3. Cut a piece of ribbon or yarn about twelve inches long.
4. Place the first set of pictures face down on the table as shown here.
5. Put glue on the back of each picture.
6. Lay the yarn down the center of each picture.
7. Place the second set of pictures on the back of the first set, matching the edges.
8. Hang in a location where the story reminds you that Jesus is the Messiah, the Savior God promised to send.

Permission to photocopy for local church use. © 2003 Abingdon Press.

WIND AND FLAME

The Bible
Acts 2:1-16

I will give my Spirit
to everyone.
(Acts 2:17, CEV)

Supplies
paper
scissors
paper punch
string or yarn

Bible Story

The day came for the Festival of Pentecost, a time of giving thanks to God. The disciples and other followers of Jesus had gathered in a house in Jerusalem to offer thanks for the first harvest.

Peter looked around at the group. "How we have grown," he thought to himself. "Since Jesus' death and resurrection, every day there are more and more of us, but we are still here in Jerusalem. We are still waiting. On that hillside in Galilee, Jesus had told us to go to all nations and make disciples. But he also promised to send us a helper. It has been many days. I wonder when it will happen."

Almost as soon as Peter had thought the words, a sound like the rush of a strong wind filled the room. Peter looked at all those who were there. What looked like flames danced above their heads. Everyone began to talk at once—but in different languages. They were all telling the story of Jesus. And what was even stranger, everyone understood.

The chattering people inside the house made so much noise that a crowd gathered in the street. "What's going on here?" they asked. "How can it be that everyone is speaking a different language, and yet we can all understand?"

That was when Peter knew what had happened. The Holy Spirit had indeed come. Everyone present would have that special power that Jesus had promised them.

Peter stood outside the house and spoke to the crowd that was gathered there. "Those of you who are worried about these people, don't be. They are not drinking too early in the morning. They are filled with great joy because the Holy Spirit has come to them."

Peter preached to the crowd that day. He told them about Jesus. Many people listened and believed. Three thousand were baptized and became followers of Jesus that day. The Holy Spirit was truly at work in the world.

I will give to everyone. (Acts 2:17) my Spirit my Spirit will give to everyone.

creative fun

1. Make a copy of the Holy Spirit spiral for each child in the class. (If possible, copy it onto red printer paper.)
2. Cut out the spiral.
3. Punch a hole in the center of the spiral where indicated.
4. Attach a piece of yarn or string through the hole.
5. Hang the spiral so that the moving air will make it spin.

Remind the children that God's Spirit came in a rush of wind and flames.

Permission to photocopy for local church use. © 2004 Abingdon Press.

PETER AND JOHN

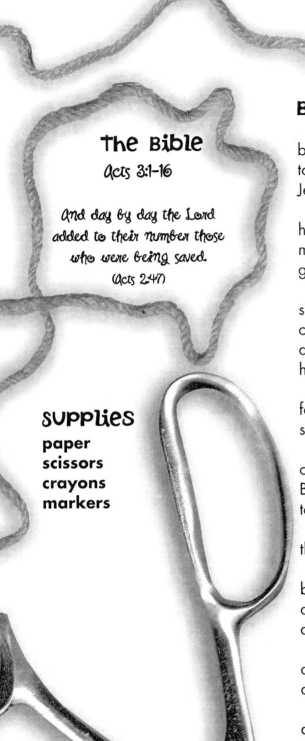

the Bible

Acts 3:1-16

And day by day the Lord added to their number those who were being saved.
(Acts 2:47)

supplies

paper
scissors
crayons
markers

Bible Story

Peter and John were two of Jesus' disciples. They had been with Jesus for a long time. They had heard what Jesus taught. They had seen Jesus heal. They had been there when Jesus had been crucified and had risen from the dead.

One day Peter and John were going to the temple at the hour of prayer. As they went into the city, they passed by a man who was sitting on a mat at the entrance to one of the gates.

The man was sitting because he could not stand. He was sitting in that particular spot because he could not walk and could not work. Every day people had to walk past him, and he could ask them for money. How lonely this man must have felt!

As Peter and John passed by, the man called out, "Alms for the poor. Help a man who cannot walk." The man stretched out his hand toward the two friends of Jesus.

Peter stopped and walked over to the man. The man held out his hands so that Peter could drop a few coins in them. But instead of handing the man coins, Peter reached out and took his right hand.

"I have no silver or gold, but what I have I give to you. In the name of Jesus Christ, get up and walk."

The man's feet and ankles grew strong. He jumped up. He began to walk. He began to run. He began to leap up and down and praise God. The people who had been standing around saw what had happened. They were amazed.

"Isn't this the man who begs for alms each day?" they asked one another. Then they began to gather around Peter and John.

"Why are you surprised?" Peter asked them. "We do not do this by our own power, but through the power of God in the name of Jesus. You did not believe that Jesus was God's Son when he was here, yet now you can see what we can do in Jesus' name." Peter and John began to tell the crowd of people about Jesus.

Peter said to him, "I have no money, but what I do have I give to you. In the name of Jesus Christ, get up and walk!"

They came across a man who was unable to walk. The man asked Peter for money for food.

Get up and walk!

The man began to walk. He began to jump. He danced with joy, praising God, and the people were amazed.

One day Peter and John were on their way to the Temple to pray.

creative fun

1. Make a copy of the storybook for each child.
2. Cut it out. Fold on the dotted lines to make a card.
3. Draw pictures that tell the story of Peter and John healing the lame man.
4. Share the story with a friend.

Permission to photocopy for local church use. © 2005 Abingdon Press.

PHILIP AND THE ETHIOPIAN

The Bible

Acts 8:26-40

How can I understand unless someone helps me?
(Acts 8:31, CEV)

Supplies

glue
paper
scissors
crayons
markers
tape
stapler, staples
paper fasteners

Bible Story

Before Jesus left the world, he told his disciples, "Go into all the world and preach the good news. Baptize those believers in my name, in God's name, and in the name of the Holy Spirit." That is just what the disciples did.

One day an angel appeared to Philip, "Leave Jerusalem. Go south to the road that goes to Gaza." The angel didn't tell him why or even what was going to happen, but Philip decided not to argue and set out on his journey.

As Philip walked along the road, a chariot drove past in a cloud of dust. Philip wished he were riding in a chariot. The man in the chariot was reading as he rolled along. A voice told Philip, "Go up to that chariot. Stay close to it."

Now Philip had to run very, very fast to keep up. The man in the chariot was a government official. He was returning from a pilgrimage to Jerusalem. When Philip finally caught up with the chariot, he could hear what the man was reading aloud. The man was reading from the book of the prophet Isaiah. Now Philip knew why the angel had sent him.

"Sir, do you know what you are reading?" Philip asked as he ran along side the chariot. The man stopped the chariot.

"How can I understand unless someone explains it to me?" the man answered. "Come up here." The man began to read.

Philip told the man, "What you are reading is the prophet Isaiah. He is telling about a Savior, a Messiah who was to come. That Savior has come. His name is Jesus. He was my friend. Let me tell you about him." And he did.

Afterwards, the man turned to Philip. "Is there any reason you cannot baptize me in that river over there?" Philip and the man climbed down from the chariot. Philip baptized this man in the name of the Lord Jesus.

Creative Fun

1. Make a copy of the Ethiopian's chariot and horse for each child.
2. Cut it out. Decorate it. Fold it on the dotted lines.
3. Tape or glue Tab A and Tab B to the sides A and B of the

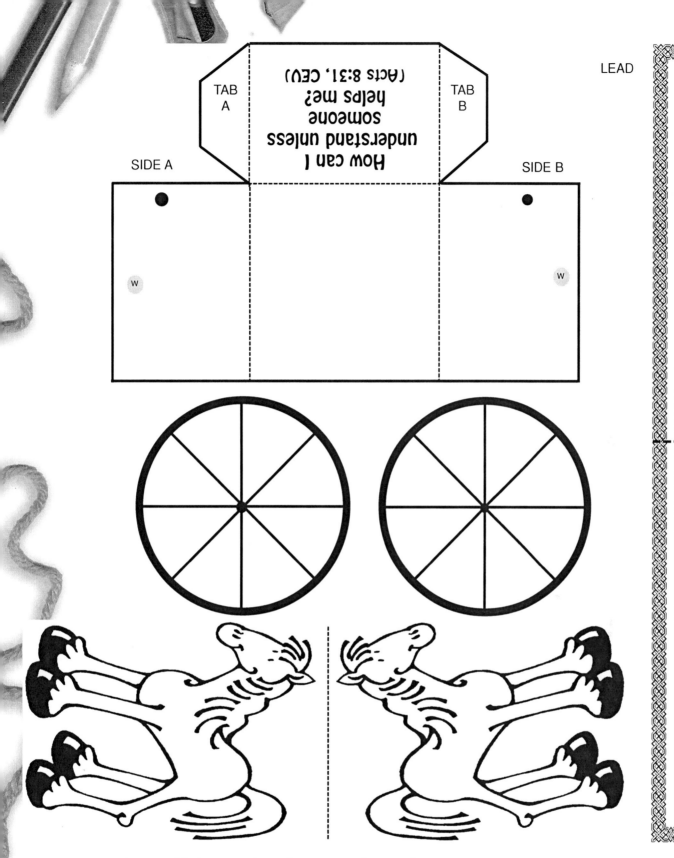

LEAD

TAB A

How can I understand unless someone helps me? (Acts 8:31, CEV)

TAB B

SIDE A

SIDE B

W

W

chariot. Make sure the tabs are on the inside.

4. Fold the horse on the dotted line. Fold the lead on the dotted line. Tape an end of the lead to each of the sides of the chariot where indicated by the dot. Sandwich the lead between the two halves of the horse. Staple.

5. Fasten the wheels at the circle marked with a "W". Read the Bible verse.

Permission to photocopy for local church use. © 1997 (horse), 2005 (chariot) Abingdon Press.

DAMASCUS ROAD

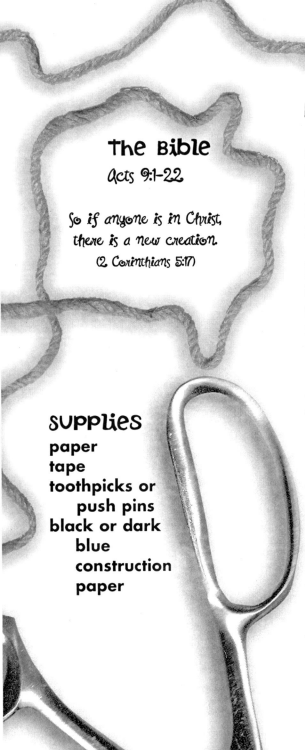

The Bible

Acts 9:1-22

So if anyone is in Christ, there is a new creation.
(2 Corinthians 5:17)

Supplies

paper
tape
toothpicks or push pins
black or dark blue construction paper

Bible story

"The followers of Jesus are troublemakers. We must get rid of them," said Saul, for he was a righteous man. So, Saul went from house to house in Jerusalem. Every follower of Jesus he found—every man, every woman, every child—he arrested and put in prison. But this was not enough for Saul, for he was a righteous man.

"Many followers of Jesus have left Jerusalem," he told the high priest. "Some of them are even preaching and teaching in Damascus. Let me go there and arrest them. I'll bring them back to Jerusalem." The high priest agreed, for he, like Saul, was a righteous man.

Saul gathered some men to go with him. They set out for Damascus. As the group got near the city, a bright light shone all around Saul. He fell down to the ground. A voice came from the light. "Saul, why are you doing this?"

"Who is this?" Saul asked. He was afraid.

"I am Jesus, the one whose followers you are hurting. Go into the city. Wait and you will be told what to do next." The men who were traveling with Saul heard the voice, but they didn't see anyone and didn't know what was going on.

Saul stood up. "Help!" he shouted. "I'm blind!" The men took Saul by the hand and led him into Damascus. For three days Saul sat in darkness. He was too upset to eat or drink. There he waited, just as Jesus had told him to.

At the same time in another part of the city, a follower of Jesus named Ananias received a message from Jesus. "Go to the place where Saul is staying. Lay your hands on him so that he might see again."

Ananias had heard about Saul. He knew that Saul hunted down Jesus' followers and arrested them, but he did as Jesus told him. He found Saul and touched him. Saul's vision returned.

For the rest of his time in Damascus, instead of hunting down Jesus' followers, Saul became one. He preached the good news about Jesus to all who would listen.

creative Fun

1. Make a copy of the pin-prick picture for each child in the class.
2. Place the picture over a piece of black or dark blue construction paper. Tape lightly at the top and bottom so that it doesn't move.
3. Using a toothpick or a push pin, poke the holes in the illustration.
4. When all the holes have been poked, remove the top picture.
5. Hold the construction paper up to the light. Saul finally saw the "light."

Permission to photocopy for local church use. © 2003 Cokesbury.

PAUL AND LYDIA

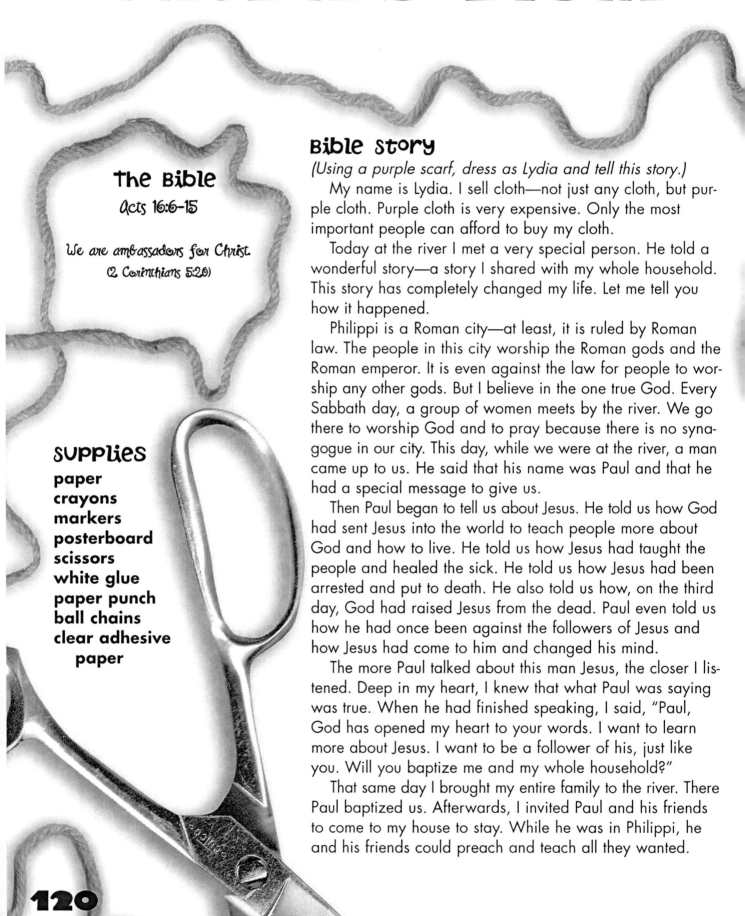

The Bible

Acts 16:6-15

We are ambassadors for Christ.
(2 Corinthians 5:20)

Supplies

paper
crayons
markers
posterboard
scissors
white glue
paper punch
ball chains
clear adhesive
   paper

Bible Story

(Using a purple scarf, dress as Lydia and tell this story.)

My name is Lydia. I sell cloth—not just any cloth, but purple cloth. Purple cloth is very expensive. Only the most important people can afford to buy my cloth.

Today at the river I met a very special person. He told a wonderful story—a story I shared with my whole household. This story has completely changed my life. Let me tell you how it happened.

Philippi is a Roman city—at least, it is ruled by Roman law. The people in this city worship the Roman gods and the Roman emperor. It is even against the law for people to worship any other gods. But I believe in the one true God. Every Sabbath day, a group of women meets by the river. We go there to worship God and to pray because there is no synagogue in our city. This day, while we were at the river, a man came up to us. He said that his name was Paul and that he had a special message to give us.

Then Paul began to tell us about Jesus. He told us how God had sent Jesus into the world to teach people more about God and how to live. He told us how Jesus had taught the people and healed the sick. He told us how Jesus had been arrested and put to death. He also told us how, on the third day, God had raised Jesus from the dead. Paul even told us how he had once been against the followers of Jesus and how Jesus had come to him and changed his mind.

The more Paul talked about this man Jesus, the closer I listened. Deep in my heart, I knew that what Paul was saying was true. When he had finished speaking, I said, "Paul, God has opened my heart to your words. I want to learn more about Jesus. I want to be a follower of his, just like you. Will you baptize me and my whole household?"

That same day I brought my entire family to the river. There Paul baptized us. Afterwards, I invited Paul and his friends to come to my house to stay. While he was in Philippi, he and his friends could preach and teach all they wanted.

creative FUN

1. Make a copy of the backpack pulls for each child in the class.
2. Decorate the pulls with bright colors.
3. Using one of the pulls as a pattern, cut two circles from posterboard.
4. Put glue on one side of the posterboard circle.
5. Place one printed circle on that side, matching the edges.
6. Put glue on the opposite side and cover with a second printed circle, matching the edges.
7. Cover the backpack pull with clear adhesive paper.
8. Trim the excess paper around the circle.
9. Punch a hole and thread a ball chain through the hole.

Permission to photocopy for local church use. © 2003 Cokesbury.

A LETTER FROM PAUL

The Bible
Acts 18:1–11;
1 Corinthians 13:4–8

Love is patient; love is kind.
(1 Corinthians 13:4)

Supplies
paper
crayons
markers
scissors
tape

Bible Story
Refrain:
A letter, a letter. Paul sent the churches letters.
He helped them know just what to do to follow
Jesus better.

One fine day in Corinth, Paul met a friendly pair.
Their names were Priscilla and Aquila; they made tents
    while there.
Together they would make their tents and teach and preach
    and pray.
When Paul moved on to Ephesus, he told his friends to stay.

Refrain

The Corinth church was growing with people every day.
They came to hear of Jesus, to worship, sing, and pray.
But members of the growing church soon began to fight.
They wanted Paul to help them know which group was really
    right.

Refrain

But Paul was still in Ephesus, a city far away.
He could not get to Corinth, but he had a lot to say.
So he wrote the folks a letter that said, "Please get along.
We're all united in the faith, don't fight about right or wrong.

Refrain

"We're baptized with one Spirit; we're one in Jesus Christ.
We're neither Jew nor Greek nor slave, but ONE in Jesus Christ.
The gifts the Lord has given you are for the common good.
So work together one and all, just like you know you should."

Refrain

"Love is patient, love is kind, neither envious nor rude.
Love provides the greatest hope, and rejoices in the truth.
Love will never pass away; there is no end to love.
Now faith and hope and love abide, but greatest of these is
    love."

creative Fun

1. Make a copy of the heart messenger for each child in the class.
2. Decorate the heart and cut it out.
3. With adult assistance, cut the two slits on the inside of the heart.
4. Cut out the Bible verse strips.
5. Tape them together, forming one long strip.
6. Thread the strip up through one of the slits in the heart and down through the other. Pull the strip to read the Bible verse.

Love is kind and patient, never jealous,

boastful, proud or rude. Love isn't selfish

or quick tempered. (1 Corinthians 13:4–5, CEV)

Permission to photocopy for local church use. © 1999 Abingdon Press.

SHIPWRECKED!

The Bible

Acts 21:27—28:15

Nothing in all creation can separate us from God's love for us in Christ Jesus our Lord!

(Romans 8:39, CEV)

Supplies

paper
scissors
crayons
markers
blue construc-
    tion paper
tape
white glue
plastic drinking
    straws
white drawing
    paper

Bible Story

Wherever Paul went, he preached the good news about Jesus. Sometimes this caused him some problems. One day he was arrested and about to be beaten by the soldiers when he shouted, "I may be a Jew, but I am also a Roman citizen. I demand to be tried by the Emperor of Rome."

Now most people didn't know that Paul was a Roman citizen, and it was indeed illegal to punish him for a crime when he had not even be tried by a Roman court. So they decided to send him to Rome. There he would have a trial.

Paul and his friends were put on board a ship that was heading for Rome. It wasn't a very good time to travel. The winds were unpredictable, and storms often came up without warning. But the council didn't care. They were rid of Paul for the time being. A great storm came up over the Mediterranean Sea. The wind howled. Waves smacked against the boat and crashed over the decks. Even the sailors on board the ship were frightened.

"We're going to drown!" the soldiers shouted. "We're going to drown!" the captain shouted. "We're going to drown!" everyone shouted—everyone except Paul.

"Don't be afraid," Paul shouted over the storm. "No one is going to die. God has promised me that we would all be safe—everyone of us." And when daylight came, the storm was over. Everyone was safe. Everyone was grateful.

But the ship was in terrible shape. The sailors looked for a safe place to make repairs to the ship, but as the ship came close to shore, it ran up onto a rocky reef and began to break apart.

"Everyone jump in and swim for shore," shouted one of the guards. "If you can't swim, grab a piece of wood and float to shore."

Just as Paul had promised, every sailor, every prisoner, and every soldier made it safely to land. They spent the winter on that island. In the spring they set sail for Rome once more. Paul was placed under house arrest there, but he continued to tell the story of Jesus Christ, even in Rome.

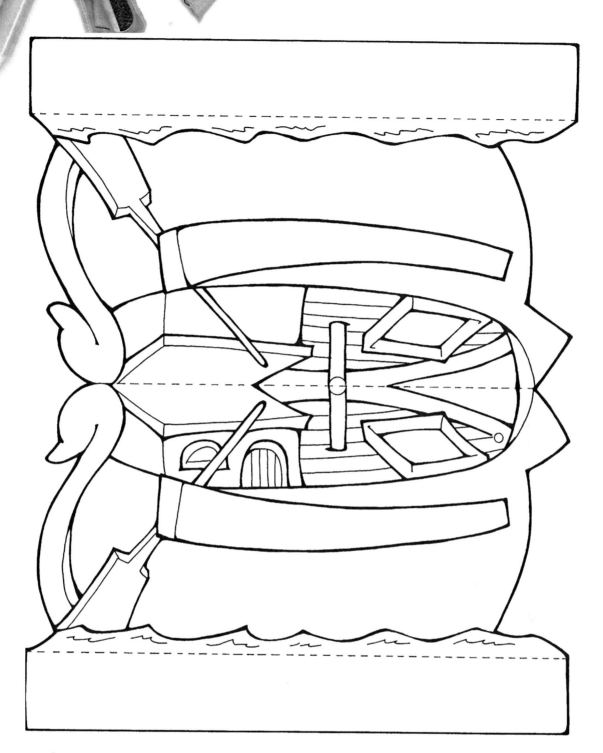

creative FUN

1. Make a copy of the Roman ship for each child in the class.
2. Color the ship and cut it out.
3. Fold the ship in half on the dotted lines.
4. Cut the hole where the mast will go.
5. Fold the base strips out.
6. Tape or glue the ship to a piece of dark blue construction paper.
7. Insert a plastic drinking straw through the hole to form a mast.
8. Cut a piece of white paper about four inches by six inches. Write the Bible verse for today on the paper. Tape the paper to the mast for a sail.

Permission to photocopy for local church use. © 1999 Abingdon Press.

SCRIPTURE INDEX

Old Testament

SCRIPTURE INDEX

New Testament

Writer: LeeDell Stickler
Development Editor: LeeDell Stickler
Production Editor: Sylvia Slack
Production and Design Manager: R.E. Osborne
Designer: Paige Easter
Illustrators: Megan Jeffery, Susan Harrison